Advance praise f

"*Marriage PATH* is a richly biblical treatment of marital peacemaking, rooted especially in Jesus' teaching in the Beatitudes. Lee's emphasis on kingdom virtues—such as humility, hope, hunger for justice and peace, and mercy—adds an extremely important dimension to Christian thinking about marriage. Deftly interweaving copious scriptural citations, personal stories and powerful anecdotes, and clinical research, Lee writes with admirable clarity and wisdom. I strongly recommend this book."

David P. Gushee, PhD
Distinguished University Professor of Christian Ethics
Mercer University
Author, *Getting Marriage Right*

"Cameron Lee explains in a clear, thoughtful, and profound manner the kingdom-oriented virtues required to be peacemakers within a Christian marriage. The case is made, chapter by chapter, for practical steps we can take to develop a perspective and vision for what God can provide to everyone: hope for restoration, and the virtues that will allow us to be peacemakers in the home and within our communities.

"This book is equally useful for personal or group study. The questions at the end of every chapter help us as Christians explore our own marriages, encourage reflection on what we yearn for, and provide a map for developing humility and compassion."

Joseph L. Hernandez, Ph.D.
Licensed Clinical Psychologist and
Marriage and Family Therapist
Author, *Family Wellness Skills*

"This book provides an insightful critique of the values many hold to be critical for a happy marriage, as shaped by the cultural messages of our day. Virtues of peace, hope, humility, righteousness, and compassion are re-envisioned, drawing upon the truth of God's Word and reconstructed within God's design for marriage. The author challenges us to re-imagine marriage as a life of discipleship in which we live out the attitudes of Christ in and through the everyday realities of our relationship. The message of peacemaking is the path to transforming our marriages from the inside out."

Helen Noh, Ph.D.
Assistant Professor of Psychology
Chair, Department of Psychology
Tyndale University and Seminary

"Is it possible that something as everyday as marriage can lead us on a path to redemption, restoration and renewal? To live in peace requires that we learn to live beyond ourselves and embrace God's grace and mercy, not only for our spouses but for ourselves as well. *Marriage PATH*, which can be read by individuals or studied in a couple or small group format, teaches readers to embrace peace and find fulfillment in marriage and family life."

Sharon Hargrave
Executive Director, Boone Center for the Family
Pepperdine University
Author, *Leader's Guide: 5 Days to a New Marriage*

Marriage
PATH

Marriage PATH

Peacemaking at Home for Christian Couples

Cameron Lee

FULLER INSTITUTE FOR
RELATIONSHIP EDUCATION
Pasadena, CA

Published by the Fuller Institute for Relationship Education
Fuller Theological Seminary, Pasadena, CA

Cover image: Anita Berghoef

Cover design: Randa K. Lee

ISBN: 0615985386
ISBN-13: 978-0615985381

To all who would make peace at home

CONTENTS

FOREWORD

Tod Bolsinger
Vice-President for Vocation and Formation
Fuller Theological Seminary

I close the car door with a thud, walk up the stairs, fumble with my keys, open the door and let my computer bag slide onto the floor, the weight of the day going with it.

From upstairs, my wife's cheery voice fills the stairway, "Welcome home, honey!" Our two retrievers bound down the stairs to greet me. My teenage daughter follows behind, smiling, and gives me a hug. "Hi Daddy. Glad you're home."

I let out a deep sigh through a smile.

I shrug off my coat, and tie on an apron. My wife hands me a glass of wine while our daughter chats via email with our son, who is away at college. We throw garlic in a pan and start chopping vegetables, making dinner together while we "say our days."

Home. I sigh and smile again thinking about it. Just to enter our house after fighting the tedious traffic-filled drive and a long day of meetings, deadlines, emails, and demands, is to enter into a different space, a different time. *Chronos* gives way to *kairos*: agendas are set aside for connections. Recapping the events since we were last together is not a report on productivity, but a sharing for renewing intimacy.

"And God saw it and it was good."

If a rabbi was sitting in our kitchen amidst that reunion routine, I believe he would gently remind us that the Bible has a great word for the contented sigh, the reflexive smile and the gentle comfort of that regular routine: *Shalom*. Peace. Not just the absence of conflict, shalom, is, as Cameron Lee reminds us in this beautiful and practical little book, "'The way things ought to be': the way things were created to be, with all the inherent and delight-giving goodness with which they were originally endowed by the Creator."

But for so many of us, this vision of a home filled with shalom is so elusive as to be taunting. Indeed, for most of my own growing up years, entering my home was walking into a vacant and bruised space where each person walked cautiously and gingerly trying to avoid the emotional trip wires.

I know personally how precious is this peace.

ꕥ

This book doesn't just offer us a vision, but a PATH (an acronym for "peacemaking at home"). Not just a picture of a family filled with peace, but the wisdom for learning and living into it that begins at the altar, in the vows of a couple who come before God and their community to make promises that will bind them until death, hoping against hope that they might actually experience the fairy-tale ending: "and they lived happily ever after."

Lee draws upon years of experience as a professor of family studies and pastor to bring together the best insights of academic research, biblical scholarship, and a life of listening deeply to the longings and losses of people to bring us back to a vision of family that is the fruit of lives and marriages tutored in Christian *virtues*.

Using the lessons of Jesus from the Sermon on the Mount, Lee doesn't offer quick fixes, but a compelling counter-vision to the trite clichés found on the covers of magazines in grocery store checkout aisles or airport newsstands. Lee takes us out of our family rooms and up onto a mountainside to hear a Teacher speak of the way the world is supposed to be.

He then descends with us right into the most intimate places of our lives. Back to kitchen tables where bills are being paid, where plans are being made, where the to-do lists of life are navigated. Lee asks necessary, good, hard questions that will take us back to the last argument, the last night when we turned over in bed and turned our backs to our beloved, the last time we felt hurt and lashed out.

For Lee, the PATH to a marriage and a family that experiences and points to God's intention for the whole world is found in the long, hard, joyful work of continually reconnecting our longing for happiness with the well-spring of virtue.

As we do, we find unanticipated paradoxes: Only as we seek the Kingdom and let go of the idol of our own happiness—even marital and family happiness—can we find peace. Only as we respond to voice of the Spirit and the word of God can we be formed into the kinds of people who truly know and give others the peace of God. Only as we set aside the mental models of a world striving for satisfaction do we find the deep shalom that God has been offering us all along.

This is not some idealistic, philosophical tome. It is a winsome, hopeful, and brutally honest and deeply *personal* re-appraisal of some of the most important ideas that most of us have long set aside.

Like the call to follow Jesus itself, the PATH to a marriage and a family filled with the peace of God will require much of us.

But what better way to spend a lifetime?

ഗ്രൂ

INTRODUCTION

When I was a kid, I owned a Bible that I never read.

It was a New Testament, actually: a pocket-sized, leather-bound edition designed for soldiers on the move. It had been given to me by my grandmother in the hopes that one day I would read it and somehow become a Christian.

I was probably around ten or twelve years old when I decided to give it a look. Not knowing what else to do, I began at the beginning, with the gospel of Matthew. Back then, most of the versions of the Bible that we now enjoy didn't exist; my little New Testament, therefore, was in King James English. Right off the bat, I was in trouble. Matthew opened with a string of people with strange names that I couldn't pronounce, who "begat" a whole bunch of other people with equally difficult names.

But somehow I persevered. Chapter 2 gave me the Christmas story of the wise men and their gifts, and the brutal King Herod: that felt at least a little familiar. The subsequent tales of John the Baptist and the temptation of Jesus were new to me, but I could read them as simply stories in their own right.

Then I hit chapter 5, the beginning of what's known as the Sermon on the Mount. Some of the teaching made a little sense; if nothing else, I could tell that Jesus was a man with something important and difficult to say.

Some of it, however, seemed rather odd.

"Blessed are the poor in spirit, for theirs is the kingdom of heaven," Jesus began, going on to say that those who mourn, who are meek, and who hunger and thirst for righteousness are also blessed. I hadn't grown up in the church, and knew nothing about the Bible. Still, this seemed to me a rather strange way of talking about blessing.

It would be years before I would become a Christian, in college. And it was years more before I would come back to try to make sense of Jesus' odd teaching about blessing and the kingdom of heaven.

Jesus has much to say about the kingdom; it was the central theme of his preaching. I've come to the conclusion that if we can begin to understand what he means by "blessing"—or, as we shall see, by a gospel redefinition of "happiness"—we'll have a better grasp on the life to which he calls us.

And that includes not just who we are in public, but who we are in private, at home, where only God and our family sees.

ꕥ

As often happens with books, this one has been a long time coming.

I had thought and taught about the Beatitudes for a long time before writing a book on the subject. That was over a decade ago, and in the years since, that seemingly odd teaching of Jesus has continued to shape my personal and professional vision.

The Beatitudes, I believe, capture much of the essence of Jesus' kingdom message, reaching a climax in the call to be "peacemakers." Jesus says that peacemakers are blessed or happy because "they will be called God's children" (Matthew 5:9). Why? Because God is a God of peace, and those who make peace in his name demonstrate the character of their heavenly Father.

Christians are called to be peacemakers in a broken world. And that includes being willing channels of God's peace at home. The more I go from place to place conducting marriage workshops, particularly in the church, the more convinced I am of the need for spiritually formative marriage instruction grounded in a peacemaking perspective. We don't just need more advice: we need vision.

The book you now hold was written with that need in mind. I've called it "Marriage PATH" not only as a metaphor for the journey of Christian discipleship in general, or of married life in particular, but as an acronym for "Peacemaking at Home." The central idea is that if we are called to follow Jesus by being peacemakers, then we must learn to do this in all of our relationships, including the ones we sometimes take for granted—our marriages and families.

Peacemaking means much more than just learning the skills of negotiation and conflict resolution. Don't get me wrong: over the years, I have taught communication and conflict skills to hundreds of couples, and am convinced that such skills have an important place.

But as marriage researcher and therapist John Gottman has observed, even the strongest, most stable couples continue to have arguments over the same old things over and over again. The difference between happy and unhappy couples, he insists, is not that the happy ones find solutions to all their problems, but that they do things to maintain an atmosphere of positivity and trust even when a problem can't be solved.[1]

Here's my concern. In a world already glutted with self-help books whose titles make lofty promises, we're asked to believe that just about any personal difficulty could be resolved with a program of three, or five, or ten simple steps. And it's true that small changes—the right ones!—can make a big difference in a relationship.

The dark side of the promise of technical solutions, however, is that couples may half-heartedly try something they heard in a workshop or read in a book, and just as quickly abandon these new behaviors if they don't immediately get the results they want. "Well, *that* didn't work," they mutter, tempted once again to write off their marriage or spouse as a hopeless case.

Christians must learn to think differently. To follow Jesus is not to be handed a set of biblical solutions to life's problems. We are called into a lifetime of discipleship, in which the ideas and attitudes native to the world we live in are replaced by those native to the kingdom of heaven, the kingdom that Jesus lived and preached—the kingdom envisioned in the Beatitudes.

It's possible to change a marriage from the outside in. When couples learn new behaviors, it opens a space for interactions that feel different and better, which in turn can provoke a shift in attitude. My goal here, however, is to work from the inside out, to foster attitudes that are grounded in a specifically Christian vision of discipleship, which are then applied to the daily reality of married life.

Thus, this is not a typical marriage "curriculum" per se, but something closer to a Bible study specifically designed to help Christians think and talk about their own marriages *as* Christians. The book presents a biblical vision of peacemaking to be embodied in marriage through the virtues of hope, hunger, humility, and compassion.

(Yes, I tried to come up with a fourth *h*—"hospitality"?—but finally decided to let it go. I think my preaching professor, God rest his soul, would have forgiven me.)

Thus, chapter 1 argues for the importance of virtue, against the background of competing and common assumptions about happiness. Chapter 2 then sketches the biblical big picture of peacemaking: God's work of restoring wholeness to a world broken by sin. As Christians, we are called to be part of that work, even in our marriages. The implications of that vision for what the Bible calls "hope" are discussed in chapter 3.

Chapter 4 suggests that those who truly understand the need for peace and who hope in God's promised future will hunger to see things put right, and will want to be part of that work themselves. That entails becoming people who make peace in our homes and marriages, by learning to be humble (chapters 5 and 6) and compassionate with our spouses, learning the importance of empathy (chapter 7) and the double movement of apology and forgiveness (chapter 8). A final epilogue pulls it all together by insisting that peacemaking is not a solitary calling, but something that must be done in Christian community.

The book is intended for both individual and group study. At the end of each chapter, you'll find a series of questions for personal reflection and/or group discussion. If you're a small group leader, I recommend that you encourage group members to read and reflect on all of the questions. Depending on the size of the group, however, you may want to choose a smaller number of questions to actually discuss, to make sure everyone has a chance to talk if they wish. You can also encourage those so inclined to write out their answers in a journal before coming to group, which will help them collect their thoughts.

Keep in mind that some of the questions are quite personal in nature. Always, always, always make sure that the group is a welcoming and safe place for spouses and couples to interact honestly and prayerfully. No one should ever feel pressured to answer a question if they don't want to do so; no one should ever feel demeaned or rejected because of the answer they've given. And confidentiality must be stringently protected: what gets said in the group should stay in the group (don't even share what you've heard as an anonymous "prayer request"!), unless specific permission is given to talk about it elsewhere.

Though I will give practical illustrations and recommendations, this book is more about perspective than behavioral strategies, about the "why" that forms the basis for the "what" and the "how." There are many excellent skill-based marriage curricula already available from other sources, including Christian and secular programs alike. This book is intended to serve a more visionary purpose: helping you as couples and congregations to move toward a shared understanding of what Christian discipleship has to do with marriage. Marriages and marriage ministries need a coherent biblical answer to the "why" before tackling the "how," and I hope this book will provide enough of a theological foundation both to critique existing curricula as well as to gratefully adopt the skills and insights they teach.

ꟿ

As is said so often in introductions like these, no book is written in a vacuum, and this one is no exception. I have been wonderfully privileged over many years to teach hundreds of seminary students whose faithfulness to God translated into a passion for working with hurting couples and families. Their passion, indeed, has helped sustain my own.

I count these former students now as colleagues, and a number have given of their time and energy to read the manuscript and offer their valuable feedback. My sincere thanks, therefore, to Dr. Anita Liu, Megan Lundgren, Barbara Millar, Jaime Nakasuji, and Kelly Sun. Your keen editorial eyes helped me know where more clarity was needed, and saved me from many errors that otherwise would have made it into print (Jaime, I'll never forget your question about whether, in one sentence, I *meant* to talk like a pirate).

Many thanks to Tod Bolsinger for writing such a beautiful and generous foreword to this book. It is a privilege to partner with you in the mission of spiritual formation. Thanks also to Pastor Seigo Takayoshi and the people of Los Angeles Holiness Church for providing a warm and welcoming venue for "test-driving" early versions of the ideas in this book. Your encouragement has been to me like a smile from God.

A shout out to my colleagues in the Department of Marriage and Family at Fuller Seminary, who over the last several years have so enthusiastically embraced peacemaking as a core tenet of what we teach: I can't imagine a more supportive team. Terry Hargrave in particular was the one who encouraged us to extend the peacemaking vision outward from the lecture hall and into the process of personal formation with our students.

But my deepest thanks go to my wife, Suha. We were both geeky 16-year-old college freshmen when we met on a Christian retreat; I was reading *The Making of Star Trek*. A little over four years later, she married me anyway (or maybe "because"?). Though we were born in different countries, there's a sense in which we grew up together: through marriage, through graduate school, through parenting. And we're not done growing yet, as we plod our way toward resurrection in these increasingly creaky bodies of ours.

I could have no better partner on the path. Thank you for who you are, who you are becoming, and the man you have helped me to be. I love you.

Pasadena, CA
February 2015

1

THE PURSUIT OF HAPPINESS

Picture, if you will, a couple named Danny and Celia, who were introduced to each other by mutual friends at church and hit it off almost immediately.[1] They had much more in common than just their spiritual beliefs. They shared the same quirky sense of humor and offbeat musical tastes—and as they quickly discovered to their great delight, they even enjoyed the same favorite drink at Starbucks. It seemed like a match made in heaven.

Their courtship was relatively brief. Less than a year into the relationship, and with the help of friends and family, Danny plotted and executed an elaborate, romantic, one-of-a-kind proposal of marriage. With a gasp and tears of joy, Celia threw her arms around his neck and said yes.

Eight months later, the wedding came off relatively smoothly. The bride and her bridesmaids were beautiful, the men appropriately groomed, the flower girl and ring bearer adorable. There was a bit of frantic uncertainty just before the ceremony as the maid of honor lost track of Danny's wedding ring. But the pastor quietly slipped his own ring into the proceedings, and everything went forward as planned, with no one the wiser.

And when at last the pastor said, "I now pronounce you husband and wife—you may kiss the bride," the congregation cheered and hooted and clapped. For the young couple, it felt like waking up into a dream that was actually coming true. It was the happiest day of both their lives.

But the storybook feeling didn't last.

They were, of course, still very much in love. And if anyone had asked, they would have said they were happy.

But privately, they began to notice little things that annoyed them. Celia liked to keep their apartment tidy and just so, in a way that felt excessive to Danny. He was used to leaving his dirty clothes lying around until there was enough for a load of laundry. He couldn't relate to Celia's need for order; she was dumbfounded that it would be so hard for him to learn to pick up his socks. Tentatively, they tried to correct each other's behavior, but the relationship felt prickly when they did. So they tried to ignore the little things instead.

They *tried.* But they still noticed, and they were still annoyed, even if they didn't say anything.

And there were hints of bigger things. Danny loved spending time with his large, boisterous, and sometimes intrusive extended family. Celia, however, was an only child from a family that tended to keep to themselves. When they were still dating, she dutifully accompanied him to his family get-togethers, but felt like she never quite fit in, like she was being tolerated for Danny's sake. Danny, for his part, had hoped that after they were married, the barrier she felt would magically disappear. It didn't. A subtle (and sometimes not so subtle) tug of war developed between them: the tension surfaced every time Danny wanted to visit his parents.

Things didn't improve when their first child came along. The pregnancy was planned, and Celia secretly hoped that the baby would draw them closer together. But she hadn't anticipated the almost spiritual connection she began to feel with the child growing inside her, and turned more and more inward as the pregnancy progressed. For Danny's family, this was the first grandchild—a momentous occasion, and cause for celebration. His parents wanted to be more involved, and the tug of war intensified. All parties felt justified in their own desires and behavior, but increasingly confused by and resentful of the behavior of others.

All of these things could be considered the normal kind of growing pains couples suffer as they learn to build a life together. But five years into the marriage, Celia found herself listening intently to an announcement at church about an upcoming marriage workshop. She didn't consult with Danny before secretly signing them up, because she already knew that if she asked, he'd hem and haw, and finally say no. *Better to ask forgiveness than permission*, she thought to herself wryly, as she wrote their contact information on the registration form. *But we're both unhappy. We need this.* Almost as an afterthought, she mentally tossed up a quick prayer: *Please, Lord, can you make him say yes?*

❧☙

When I teach marriage workshops, I sometimes begin with a question: "Why are you here today?" Sometimes, I ask rhetorically, knowing that people may be reluctant to give honest answers in a roomful of relative strangers.

But I know that many of them are there because, in one way or another, they're unhappy in their marriage. And they want to find a way to be happier.

That's not a bad thing, as far as it goes. I'm not one to dismiss such a goal as intrinsically "unspiritual," as if the Christian life had nothing to do with happiness. I believe that a good and gracious God, as our heavenly Father, wants his children to be happy.

So if you're reading this book because you're looking for a way to have a happier marriage and a more peaceful home, I'm all for it.

Really.

But here's the catch (you knew there had to be one, didn't you?). The reason I ask the question in the first place is because the pursuit of happiness is often too shallow a reason to sustain couples in the hard and often sacrificial work they need to do in their marriage.

Many couples go searching for self-help books and workshops, looking for strategies to "fix" their relationships. And they may actually try those strategies for a time.

Sooner or later, however, the techniques seem to fail: they just don't give the hoped-for result. At that point, the temptation is to say, *Well, I guess* ***that*** *didn't work*, and give up.

I want couples to do more than look for strategies to help them feel better in their marriages: I want them to catch a larger vision of godly marriage that will keep them going through the ups and downs. I want them to have a reason to persevere, not only through the inevitable stumbles of married life, but through the awkwardness of trying new ways to think and behave.

I'll say it again—I believe that God wants his children to be happy, and hope that this book will in some way shed light on the path. The problem isn't with happiness itself. It's with the typical and mistaken ways we think about happiness and how to achieve it.

The plan for this first chapter, therefore, is to take a good hard look at happiness. In recent decades, a great deal of research has been done on what makes people happy, and some of the results may surprise you. So please bear with me if at points the discussion seems too academic. I want to show you, on the basis of both Scripture and psychological research, why we need to rearrange our mental furniture, to change our way of thinking, in order to open a space for what I hope is a more biblical way of approaching marriage.

Don't just make your marriage happier; understand the kind of person God is calling you to be.

Thus, we'll begin with a summary of the research on happiness and well-being, then turn to what the Bible has to say, concentrating on the text which inspired this book: the Beatitudes at the beginning of Jesus' Sermon on the Mount (Matthew 5:3-12). What Jesus teaches about true happiness will provide the vision we need to do what must be done in our homes.

To put the matter simply: don't just look for ways to make your marriage happier; understand the kind of person God is calling you to be, look for ways to put that into practice, and keep doing it even if you don't immediately get the results for which you hoped.

What Makes Us Truly Happy?

A vast research literature has sprung up on the related subjects of human happiness and positive emotion, and the results are instructive, sometimes even counterintuitive. We might think we know what will make us lastingly happy, but studies suggest that many of us haven't a clue.

Here are some of the surprises.

We're not very good at predicting how we will feel in the future. As humans, we think about the future all the time: if not the distant future, then at least the immediate one, anticipating from moment to moment what will happen next. When we get it right, we simply go on our way undisturbed. It's only when our expectations are violated that we may notice that we even had expectations at all.

When it comes to our emotions, as Daniel Gilbert has argued, we're not good at predicting how happy (or unhappy) we'll be in the future.[2] Ask people how much they'd enjoy eating a cheese Danish tomorrow, and they'll base their prediction on how they'd feel about it today. If they're hungry at the time, that imaginary pastry looks pretty good; if they've just eaten and feel full, not so much.

Thus, when we're in happy circumstances, tomorrow looks rosy; in unhappy circumstances, bleak. We find it difficult to imagine that things will feel much differently than they do now.

But we're often wrong. The next point is one of the reasons why.

Changes in our circumstances don't usually account for much, because we adapt. Imagine arriving at work one morning and being called into your supervisor's office. *Uh-oh*, you think to yourself; *am I in some kind of trouble? What did I do?* But instead, the news is good—your supervisor appreciates your hard work and has given a good report on your behalf. Your next paycheck will show a substantial raise.

Would that make you happy?

Probably. Suddenly, you imagine doing the things you couldn't afford before: taking your dream vacation, buying that new car you've been coveting since your neighbor got one, or moving to a bigger house.

But soon, the vacation is over, the new car smell is gone, and the house feels crowded all over again. Your expenses have expanded, your expectations have changed, and what at first felt like a godsend is the new normal. The raise, once novel, is yesterday's news; what made you happy at first is now taken for granted. You're not *less* happy than before, but truth be told, you're not *more* happy either, or at least not much.

Scholars call this *the hedonic treadmill.*[3] Like hamsters on a wheel, we may expend a lot of effort trying to "get somewhere" in life, thinking that positive changes in circumstances will make us happy. And they will—but only for a limited time. Eventually, we get used to the change, and find out we haven't moved as far as we had hoped. (The good news is that we adapt to negative changes too, though perhaps neither as much nor as readily.[4])

People sometimes joke that they would be happy "if only" they could win the lottery. But the true stories of lives utterly ruined by such a windfall are no laughing matter.[5] It's true that poverty and financial stress can make you *un*-happy; but beyond a certain threshold (some say an annual income of about $75,000), more money seems to add nothing to emotional well-being.[6]

Well, then, if not even winning the lottery will make us happy, what will?

Think of all the ways you might complete the sentence, "If only ___, then I would be happy." The images with which we are bombarded by our ad-heavy consumer culture tempt us to believe that we can become happy by raising our standard of living, improving our looks, and so on. And again, it's true that such things can give us pleasure for a while.

But all in all, averaging across many studies, social psychologist Sonja Lyubomirsky estimates that "life circumstances and situations put together account for only about 10 percent in how happy different people are."[7]

Ten percent. Think about it. That's not much when you consider the amount of energy people devote to changing their circumstances in the pursuit of happiness.

Happiness seems more and more elusive. So again, what *does* explain differences in happiness? Brace yourself.

The number one reason why some people are happier seems to be genetic inheritance. Relax. That doesn't mean people are simply born happy or unhappy and stay that way. But research does suggest that people are predisposed to different levels of positive emotion.

Maybe you bounce out of bed in the morning, ready to face each new day with a smile. Maybe you just grumble and pull the covers over your head. And maybe you're one way, and your spouse is the other—and both of you are perplexed. Instead of criticizing each other for being either a clueless Pollyanna or an annoying Grumpy Gus, you might start by allowing that both of you may be normal.

Different, yes—but normal.

Please note, we're not talking about clinical extremes like mania or depression. But like it or not, how much positive emotion one experiences in life is to some extent genetically determined. Based on studies of sets of twins, researchers suggest that each of us has a *happiness set point* that functions like the setting on a thermostat.[8] We may run hot or cold as feelings of happiness fluctuate up or down. But they soon return to baseline, a partial explanation of the treadmill effect.

Lyubomirsky estimates that fully half of the differences in human happiness can be traced to genetic influences. That may seem like a lot. But as Lyubomirsky herself encourages, "50 percent is a long way from 100 percent."[9]

There are still things we can and should do.

☙❧

Though the general ideas of a genetic happiness set point and the hedonic treadmill are widely accepted, they're not completely uncontroversial.[10] Whatever the scholarly debate, however, two basic points remain. First, the things we typically believe will make us happy may not, or not for long. And second, we have less control over our happiness than we might wish.

But that doesn't mean we have *no* control whatsoever. It's simple math: even if genetics accounts for about 50 percent, and circumstances, only 10, that still leaves 40 percent. The choices we make matter.

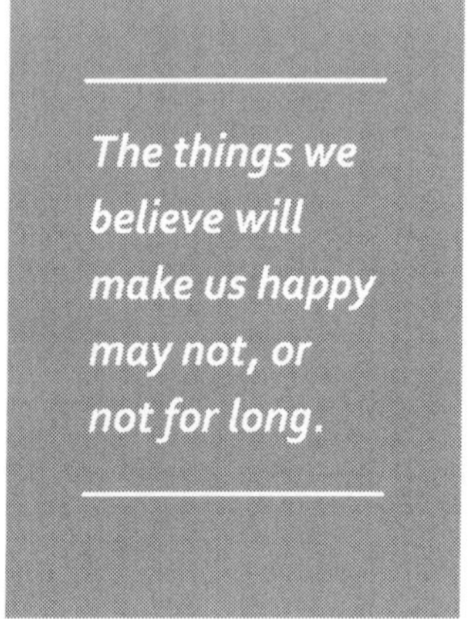
The things we believe will make us happy may not, or not for long.

As we'll see below, the moral message that comes out of the scientific literature is stunningly different than the one we get from consumer culture. It's this: if you want to be lastingly happy, then, among other things, learn to be grateful, kind, and forgiving. Set aside time and energy for nurturing positive relationships.[11]

In other words, true happiness—surprise!—just might be a matter of virtue and character.

Virtue Won't Hurt You

It's important to recognize the ways in which secular research points to a deeper moral vision of happiness. In fact, Martin Seligman, who has devoted much of his career to the development of what has become known as *positive psychology,* ironically admits that he doesn't much care for the word "happiness."[12] To him, the word too easily connotes a superficial Smiley-face kind of cheeriness.

He prefers a more classical way of thinking, in which happiness is inseparable from the moral question of what makes for a good life, for a life people would agree has been lived well. Replacing the concept of happiness with the broader construct of "well-being," Seligman looked for the goals people pursue in life for their own sake.

He proposes five of them.[13] Not surprisingly, first on the list is *positive emotion.* That is, after all, what people usually mean when they say they're happy.

But the second is what Seligman calls *engagement.* Have you ever been so engrossed in an activity that you forget to eat, or lose track of time? That's the experience known as *flow*—when the challenge of a task is so well matched to your abilities that you are completely absorbed in it.[14] This, too, is part of well-being, which will be evident to anyone who has had the privilege of experiencing it.

Third, people need a sense of *meaning* and purpose that allows them to feel part of something bigger than themselves. Fourth, they need experiences that confer a sense of competence or mastery, which Seligman calls *accomplishment.* And last but by no means least, well-being includes having *positive relationships* with others.

Each of these five goals is supported by the deliberate exercise of moral traits that Seligman calls *signature strengths.*[15] Each strength, in turn, is a route to one of six *virtues* that Seligman and his colleagues discovered in their review of "every major religious and cultural tradition."[16] Below is a list of the six proposed virtues and, in italics, their supporting strengths. Ponder these for a moment:

- Wisdom and knowledge: *curiosity; love of learning; judgment; ingenuity; social intelligence; perspective*
- Courage: *valor; perseverance; integrity*
- Humanity and love: *kindness; loving*
- Justice: *citizenship; fairness; leadership*
- Temperance: *self-control; prudence; humility*
- Transcendence: *appreciation of beauty; gratitude; hope; spirituality; forgiveness; humor; zest* [17]

It isn't necessary to define all the terms (refer to the books cited in the notes if you're interested). But imagine asking a panel of psychologists and social scientists, "What is the path to well-being and lasting happiness?" What answer would you expect? Chances are it would be somewhat different than the list above. Seligman's answers are the kind that a moral philosopher—and perhaps even the *mothers* of moral philosophers—would love.

The pursuit of money and possessions, then, is not the path to happiness, no matter what the commercials say.

And in a sense, neither is marriage. That's not saying that marriage isn't "good for you" in some ways. Being married appears to confer a wide range of potential benefits, from the consolidation of wealth to better health (especially for men who won't go to the doctor unless lovingly pestered by a concerned wife).[18]

And it's not that getting married won't make you happier—temporarily. But eventually, the adaptation/treadmill effect kicks in. As Lyubomirsky writes, citing a study that followed hundreds of married people for 15 years:

> [M]arriage has only a temporary effect on happiness. It appears that after the wedding husband and wife get a happiness boost for about two years and then simply return to their baseline in happiness, their set point. It seems wise not to share this bit of news with newlyweds.[19]

Frankly, I'm not sure I agree with that last bit of tongue-in-cheek advice. Newlyweds like Danny and Celia need realistic expectations of marriage. Think about it: when people say, "The honeymoon is over," they usually do so with regret, as if the honeymoon should (or even could!) last forever. It doesn't. But that's not saying that the new couple is unhappy. They may just be getting down to business.

Again, that doesn't mean that it's wrong or unreasonable to hope for happiness in marriage. But we need to have our values and priorities straight. To say "If only I were married, then I'd be happy" makes marriage the means to my own personal end of happiness.

There's only one small step from that thought to this one: "My spouse's job is to make me happy." Then, when disappointment inevitably strikes, we may be tempted to lament, "If only I had married *the right person*, then I'd be happy." No doubt, if we had married someone else, our situation would be *different*. But need we say more about the role of circumstances? Changing them guarantees nothing.

And more importantly, that kind of "if only" attitude treats not only the marriage as a means to an end, but our spouses themselves. This dishonors their fundamental worth as living, breathing human beings created in the image and likeness of God.

The idea of marriage as a route to personal happiness, unfortunately, is deeply embedded in modern western culture. Blaine Fowers has argued that many of us have internalized an attractive but sometimes unrealistic story of "falling in love and finding fulfillment in a love relationship."[20] He offers a more virtue-centered alternative:

> The dominant story of marriage places too much emphasis on the emotional aspects of marriage, particularly on whether the marriage is satisfying. …I have become convinced that strong marriages are built on the virtues or character strengths of the spouses. In other words, the best way to have a good marriage is to be a good person.[21]

Now *there's* an idea you're not likely to find dominating the self-help section of a bookstore. Want a good marriage? Be a good person.

It's important to not misunderstand what Fowers is proposing. Virtue isn't a new and better technique for having a happy marriage. As a marriage educator myself, I teach ideas and skills that help couples short-circuit their negative interaction patterns and build more positive ones. But Fowers is suggesting something deeper. He wants us to see the bigger picture.

Virtue, therefore, is not a method for getting what we want in life, nor for earning God's favor. It is rather the day-to-day embodiment of personal qualities—not merely behaviors, but also attitudes and dispositions—that reflect our deepest moral convictions about what life should be, about what it was meant to be.

And for followers of Jesus, this means learning to see the world as he did. If we're committed to godly marriage, we'll need to develop a biblical vision of life, which may necessitate changing how we think about happiness.

Happiness Redefined

We haven't always thought of happiness in the feeling-centered way we do today. The word "happy" originally meant something more like "lucky," as when fortune smiled upon a person by "happenstance." To some extent, happiness was a matter of fate, even providence. Consider, for example, this definition of "happy" from an early-19th-century edition of *Webster's Dictionary*:

> The pleasurable sensations derived from the gratification of sensual appetites render a person temporarily happy; but he only can be esteemed really and permanently happy, who enjoys peace of mind in the favor of God.[22]

Positive emotions are acknowledged, rather than dismissed. But they are viewed as fleeting states of pleasure. There is another kind of happiness to be desired, something more durable. It comes not from gratification but from standing in God's favor.

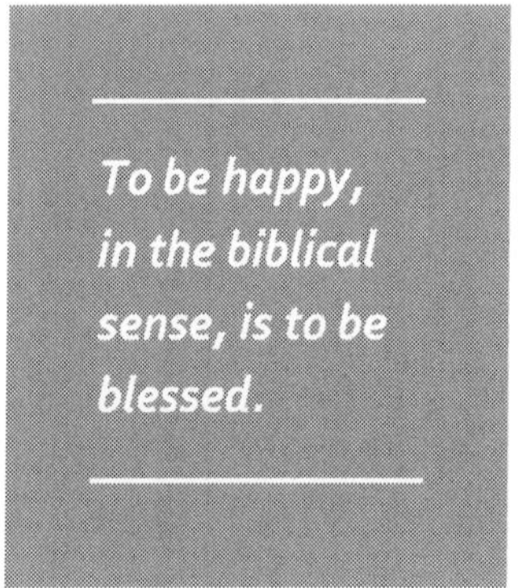
To be happy,
in the biblical
sense, is to be
blessed.

A similar way of thinking can be found in the Bible. To be happy, in the biblical sense of the word, is to be blessed. Psalm 1, for example, teaches that the those who are truly wise are blessed, because they follow the path laid out by *Torah.* Some Bibles translate *Torah* as "Law," but that's too narrow, given the way a modern ear would usually hear that word. The meaning is closer to "teaching" or "instruction":

> The truly happy person doesn't follow wicked advice, doesn't stand on the road of sinners, and doesn't sit with the

> disrespectful. Instead of doing those things, these persons love the LORD's Instruction, and they recite God's Instruction day and night! They are like a tree replanted by streams of water, which bears fruit at just the right time and whose leaves don't fade. Whatever they do succeeds. –Psalm 1:1-3

The first psalm sets the tone for the entire collection. The psalmist sets us down at a spiritual fork in the road and asks us to choose: *Which way will you go? Left or right, wickedness or wisdom? Only God's way is wise; only God's way leads to a deeply rooted and well nourished life of flourishing and fruitfulness. Follow his graciously given Instruction. Study it. Memorize it. Recite it out loud, day and night. Learn to love it.*

Jesus, of course, knew the Psalms. He quoted them constantly, even with his dying breath (e.g., Mark 15:34; Psalm 22:1). What we know as "the Old Testament" was for Jesus the *only* testament, or to use Philip Yancey's phrase, "the Bible Jesus read."[23] He understood his own life and mission to be the continuation of a story that was already in progress (e.g., Matthew 5:17-18); his thinking was shaped by the Psalms and other Old Testament traditions. We must keep this in mind when we read the New Testament, or else some of what Jesus says about happiness may be downright confusing.

Try this. Think of happiness as meaning nothing more than good feelings. Then, read the verses below, from the beginning of Jesus' Sermon on the Mount, and see if they make sense:

> Happy are people who are hopeless, because the kingdom of heaven is theirs.
> Happy are people who grieve, because they will be made glad.
> Happy are people who are humble, because they will inherit the earth.
> Happy are people who are hungry and thirsty for righteousness, because they will be fed until they are full.
> Happy are people who show mercy, because they will

receive mercy.
Happy are people who have pure hearts, because they will see God.
Happy are people who make peace, because they will be called God's children.
Happy are people whose lives are harassed because they are righteous, because the kingdom of heaven is theirs. –Matthew 5:3-10

Some of it, perhaps, makes sense, if we think in terms of the wisdom perspective of Psalm 1 discussed earlier. Wise and godly people, we can easily imagine, should be humble and merciful. They should be pure of heart, and have habits of peace. And because of such virtues, they would be blessed with divine favor.

But hopelessness and grief, hunger and harassment? These are not words we would normally associate with happiness. It doesn't even sound like God's blessing for the wise. Is Jesus saying that we need to be hopeless to be happy?

To understand what Jesus is saying, we need to delve into a different part of the Bible he read: not just the Psalms, but the prophets, particularly the prophet Isaiah.

By way of introduction, consider this story about Jesus and John the Baptist, as told in the gospel of Matthew.

John is heralded by the Jewish people as a prophet, one divinely commissioned to deliver God's word. But John had also angered the ruler Herod Antipas by condemning his adulterous relationship with his half-brother's wife (Matthew 14:1-4).[24] Herod had therefore thrown John into prison (and would later have him executed).

John is a prophet, a relative of Jesus, and the one who went before him proclaiming God's kingdom, and Jesus himself as the Lamb of God (John 1:29). But in prison, he seems to have doubts: things are not turning out as he expected. So he sends some of his own disciples to Jesus with a poignant question: "Are you the one who is to come, or should we look for another?" (Matthew 11:2-3).

Jesus *is* the one. But what answer should he give? Would

something like, "Yes, John, I'm really the Messiah, so take heart," be appropriate? Perhaps. But that's not what he says:

> Jesus responded, "Go, report to John what you hear and see. Those who were blind are able to see. Those who were crippled are walking. People with skin diseases are cleansed. Those who were deaf now hear. Those who were dead are raised up. The poor have good news proclaimed to them. Happy are those who don't stumble and fall because of me."
>
> –Matthew 11:4-6

It might sound like Jesus is saying, "Just tell John about all the miraculous things you see. That's all the answer he needs." But if that's the case, then why include, "The poor have good news proclaimed to them"? What does that have to do with anything?

Jesus is echoing the words of the prophet Isaiah. He knows that the phrases he uses will resonate with John, renewing his faith and stimulating his imagination. Here, for example, is one passage in which Isaiah describes the day in which God will finally come to save his people:

> Then the eyes of the blind will be opened, and the ears of the deaf will be cleared. Then the lame will leap like the deer, and the tongue of the speechless will sing. –Isaiah 35:5-6

And here is another, from Isaiah 61:1-3 (emphasis added):

> The LORD God's spirit is upon me, because the LORD has anointed me. *He has sent me to bring good news to the poor*, to bind up the brokenhearted, to proclaim release for captives, and liberation for prisoners, to proclaim the year of the LORD's favor and a day of vindication for our God, to comfort all who mourn, to provide for Zion's mourners, to give them a crown in place of ashes, oil of joy in place of mourning, a mantle of praise in place of discouragement.

This is in fact the passage from which, earlier in his ministry, Jesus had read aloud in his hometown synagogue, adding, "Today, this scripture has been fulfilled just as you heard it" (Luke 4:16-21). Everyone took the reading as prophetic encouragement—the day of God's favor and vindication has come! They looked upon Jesus, the carpenter's son, with wonder, and praised him for his gracious eloquence (vs. 22).

That is, until he dared to criticize them for thinking that the message of grace was meant only for them. Then they "ran him out of town" and tried to toss him over a cliff (vss. 28-29).

Even Jesus had his unpopular sermons.

If we were steeped in the Bible Jesus read, as both he and John most certainly were, then we might hear the message to his imprisoned cousin more like this: "John, think about what's happening: the things you've witnessed yourself, the things your own disciples report. The blind see and the deaf hear. The lame walk and lepers are cured. The dead are raised. *And* the gospel is preached to the poor. You know the prophecy. This is the place, and now is the time—the year of God's favor, the day of God's vindication. It's just as you announced, it's just as I preached: the kingdom of heaven is indeed at hand."

God, in other words, is beginning what he promised, right here, right now, in the ministry of Jesus. *That* is the good news that makes sense of the Beatitudes.

It's good news for the hopeless (more literally, the "poor in spirit")—for those who are victims of poverty and injustice, and have therefore given up on life.

It's good news for those who grieve, for those who are downcast because of the sin that is rampant everywhere about them, and who repent of their own sin as well. Isaiah's words were intended to encourage God's people as they mourned the loss of their land and inheritance due to their own disobedience.

It's good news for those who are humble and meek. They're not considered blessed for having shy and self-effacing personalities! These are the powerless, who have been humbled and humiliated by their history and circumstances.

And it's good news for those who hunger and thirst for righteousness. These are not people who are trying to be moral superstars through following religious rules. In the Bible, the word translated "righteousness" is often synonymous with "justice." The hungry and thirsty, therefore, are those who see all too clearly what's wrong, and long to have God put things right.

Why is it good news? Why should any of these people be considered happy or blessed? Because with Jesus, God's kingdom has come. "The kingdom of heaven *is* theirs," Jesus says twice—present tense. The day of God's salvation has already begun. But it's not complete yet, for the rest of the promises are given in the future tense: "theirs is" becomes "they will." They will…what? They will eventually see the full result of God's redemptive work.

With Jesus,
God's kingdom
has come.

People who are hopeless and poor in spirit, who grieve the sin and brokenness of the world, who have been trampled, bullied, or just plain ignored—these are the ones who hunger most to see God make everything right. He's the only one who can, and the good news of the kingdom is that the work has already begun. In time, all will be made right again. All will be as it should be.

We need to have the vision of Jesus for the good news to be good, to understand what it means to be happy and blessed. It may seem that the world has spun out of control, but God is still sovereign.

And nothing God starts will be left unfinished.

Virtue Revisited

Fowers defines the virtues as "character strengths that make it possible for human beings to pursue uniquely human aims or goods successfully."[25] But the qualities described in the first part of the Beatitudes doesn't sound much like character strengths. That's because Jesus isn't teaching his followers to take up hopelessness, grieving, and the like as self-improvement projects.

These initial Beatitudes, in other words, aren't about things we need to do to earn God's blessing, but about the surprising grace of the God who saves those who have nothing going for them. It's not about us; it's about God. But by extension, it's also about God's kingdom, the central theme of Jesus' preaching ministry and the point of his demonstrations of healing power.

For example, many of us, who have committed the Lord's Prayer to memory, have learned to pray, "Thy kingdom come. Thy will be done on earth as it is in heaven" (Matthew 6:10, King James Version). We pray for God's sovereign will to be done perfectly in every place. We pray for him to be the true and reigning king not merely in title but in the actual conduct of daily life on this earth.

The prayer continues. Having begun by calling God our Father, having addressed his name as holy ("hallowed"), we are led to consider the call to holiness in our own lives:

> Forgive us for the ways we have wronged you,
> just as we also forgive those who have wronged us.
> And don't lead us into temptation,
> but rescue us from the evil one. –Matthew 6:12-13

In other words, if we are going to pray honestly and fervently for God's will to be done, we will also have to pray for God's forgiveness and help with temptation, for we know full well that we have rebelled against his sovereignty in our own lives.

This is where the cultivation of virtue comes in. It's impossible to offer that prayer transparently without also praying, "And Lord, show me how you want me to be part of it all." We are called to a life of virtue; to hunger without hypocrisy for God's justice is to seek to become a just person oneself. The hopeless and humble, standing on God's mercy, turn outward and cultivate the attitude needed to extend mercy themselves, even in their homes. Those who catch glimpses of God's work of peace commit themselves to be agents of that peace, even in their marriages.

Happiness, therefore, is not the end toward which we aim in this life, not even in our marriages. Again, I'm *not* saying that happiness is a bad or unspiritual thing in itself to desire; the Bible, in fact, has its own vision of heavenly bliss. But as one author has written, "Happiness is not something that you can find, acquire, or achieve directly. You have to get the conditions right and then wait."[26]

The Christian life is not about the pursuit of happiness as we commonly know it, but about seeking God's kingdom (Matthew 6:33). And I am convinced that the Beatitudes offer a compelling kingdom-oriented vision of peacemaking that helps us to "get the conditions right." The vision must give rise to the virtues we must practice to transform our marriages.

Other texts than the Beatitudes, of course, will also be used; as we have already seen, for example, we can't fully understand Jesus' words if we don't hear how they echo the Psalms and the prophets. But as Glen Stassen and David Gushee have suggested,

> the virtues Jesus teaches in the Beatitudes are echoed in Paul's letters and are deeply rooted in the whole Bible. They are not merely an arbitrary selection; they are the heart of biblical virtues.[27]

In the coming chapters, I will offer hope, hunger, humility, and compassion as core virtues that derive from the Beatitudes. Each helps round out a biblical vision of marriage that is founded on the calling to be peacemakers in our own homes. But to begin, we need to look at what the Bible means by "peace."

❧☙

Questions for discussion and reflection:

(Note: if needed, please see the introduction for basic suggestions regarding small group process)

1. Think back to the story of Danny and Celia, and recall the earliest years of your own marriage. In what way, if at all, do you relate to their tale of being less and less happy as time went on? If your happiness took a turn for the worse, to what did you attribute it at the time? What would you say now?

2. How do you react to the idea that circumstances only account for a small portion of happiness, or that much more is explained by genetics?

3. Look again at Seligman's list of virtues and character strengths. What items on that list remind you of biblical teaching? How? Is there anything about the list that surprises you, or makes you think differently about happiness? Explain.

4. Respond to Blaine Fowers' statement, "the best way to have a good marriage is to be a good person." Do you agree? If so, how would you explain the idea to someone else? And what, specifically, would it mean for *you*, in your marriage?

5. Reflect on the words of the Lord's Prayer (Matthew 6:9-13). What does it mean to you to pray for God's kingdom to come? What are the implications for your own life, and for the life of the church—and particularly, for your marriage?

2

IMAGINING PEACE

As we saw in chapter 1, Christians are called to do something different than merely pursue happiness: we are called to seek God's kingdom. Jesus' Beatitudes provide us a kingdom-oriented vision of peacemaking and a set of related virtues that can transform relationships. But as of yet, I've said little about peace itself. If Jesus is calling us to be peacemakers, then we'll need to picture peace as the Bible does.

ꕥ

Born in the late 1950s, I grew up in the tumultuous decades of the 60s and 70s. It was the height of a confusing and unpopular war in South Vietnam, with protestors calling for the United States to get out. A peace movement took root in the younger generation.

In 1969, John Lennon, together with his wife Yoko Ono and their Plastic Ono Band, gave the movement something of a theme song with "Give Peace a Chance." Peace symbols were in fashion, popping up everywhere: bumper stickers, psychedelic posters, badges, even the sides of Volkswagens. To make sure everyone knew how cool I was, I wore a cheap-looking plastic peace pendant on a leather thong, even though I knew nothing about the war.

Here we are, decades later. In too many places and for too many reasons, the world is still at war. Perhaps it always has been. The pages of the Old Testament are filled with war and conquest. In the

New Testament world of the Roman Empire, violence was always on the horizon, and Jesus seemed bent on teaching his disciples that love for one's enemies, not war and strife, was the way of the kingdom (e.g., Matthew 5:43-45). And perhaps the world will always be at war, at least until Jesus returns: he himself seemed to tell his disciples as much (Matthew 24:6-8). It's no surprise, therefore, that "Make peace, not war" remains a popular slogan.

But is there more to peace than ending war?

We often think of peace in largely negative terms: peace is the *absence* of things we don't want. Indeed, what is arguably the most iconic of John Lennon's post-Beatle songs, 1971's *Imagine*, aptly illustrates this. Lennon asks us to picture a world in which people live in unity. What would such a world look like?

For starters, the lyrics suggest, people would live only for today—because they would stop believing in a future that involved either heaven or hell. And people would live in peace—because the national identities and religious beliefs for which people fight and die would be thrown out as well.

Lennon does have a point: peace is, in part, the absence of the negative. If I could snap my fingers and make people stop killing each other in the name of whatever god they serve, I would. But it saddens me to think that Lennon could only imagine heaven as part of the problem rather than the heart of the solution, the core of a vision of true peace.

Is the negative aspect of peace all there is? Sometimes, for example, when we're facing a difficult decision, we ask others to pray for us, to pray that God would "give us peace." But what does that mean? Is peace just the absence of uncertainty, of that anxiety we feel about making the wrong decision? Or is it something more?

Maybe, every now and again, we enjoy a walk along the beach or in the cool shade of a forest. What makes it peaceful? Is it just the chance to get away *from* something, or *to* something?

Biblically, it's both/and. Peace is not merely the absence of the negative, but the presence of the positive. To pray for God's peace may begin with the wish to be worry-free, but ultimately, what we really want is to be filled with serenity.

Likewise, we may go to the beach or the forest to get away from the stress and pressure of our daily routine. But we also go because we enjoy the tang of the salt air and the wind on our faces, the rhythmic roar of the surf or the gentle rustling of leaves.

Something similar can be said for the peace we desire in our homes and relationships. We want to get rid of the hurtful negativity, whether that means to stop the bickering, or to bridge the cold distance that yawns between us. We want to be free of the festering resentments that eat away at our souls. We want to end the verbal sparring, the pointed innuendos, the jokes we make at each other's expense with pretend innocence.

We want…well, what *do* we want, stated in terms of something positive? The fact is that we find it much easier to say what we *don't* want than what we *do* want.[1]

Ask yourself right now: if you want peace in your marriage, how would you know if you had it? What differences do you imagine? Don't just think of what you or your spouse would *stop* doing—think of what things you would both *do* instead.

Do we truly desire peace—real peace, God's peace? If so, then we'll need to set our sights on something more than just a cessation of hostility. As Ken Sande and Tom Raabe have written, we'll need to stop being "peace-fakers" who avoid confrontation and live in denial, or "peace-breakers" who lash out in anger.[2] Instead, we must become peace-makers (Matthew 5:9), actively doing good and pursuing the things that make for peace (Psalm 34:14).

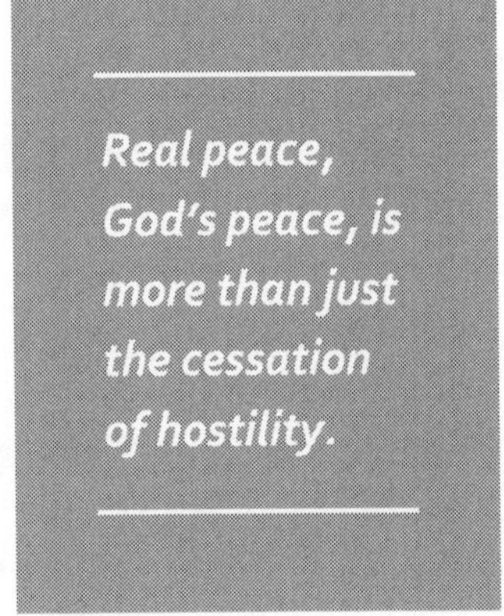

Real peace,
God's peace, is
more than just
the cessation
of hostility.

In the coming chapters, we'll take a look at four things that help make for peace in our marriages: hope, humility, a hunger to do what's right, and compassion. But first, to be sustained in the tough and often self-sacrificial work of peacemaking, we need to understand the big picture. We need to imagine peace the way the Bible does.

The Way Things Were Meant to Be

The Bible is in one sense a diverse collection of many books, but each in its own way taps into a single story of what God has done in the past, is doing now, and will do in the future. The story begins with God's creation of the universe and of humankind. Each day, God looked at what he had created, and saw that it was "good." Let's pause for a moment to consider what this might mean.

My wife and I are generally pretty conscientious about how we eat. We do almost all of our own cooking, and eat out only occasionally. Even when we do visit a restaurant, we read the menu carefully and try to make healthy choices.

But then someone gave us gift cards to The Cheesecake Factory.

After spending a good long time looking up and down the menu of three *dozen* choices of cheesecake flavors, we each made a selection and carted our prizes home.

Diet-conscious or not, we still enjoy a good dessert. Most of the time, when we have a bite of something sweet, we just smile and say, "Mmm, that's good."

But that first bite of specialty *cheesecake*? You know how it goes. We looked at each other wide-eyed, then rolled our heads back, eyes blissfully closed as we slowly savored that sweet, creamy richness. "Wow," we said. "That's good. That's *reallllly* good."

Now, obviously, there's no cheesecake mentioned in Genesis 1.

But what do we imagine when we read the creation story? Do we picture an aloof and disinterested Creator who just goes through the motions? One who says "good" the way a quality-control manager might declare that proper procedures had been followed?

Or dare we imagine a God who actually *delighted* in creation?

On the sixth and final day, God made human beings—male and female—in his image, and gave them dominion over the earth and its creatures. Then, looking back over all that he had created, God declared it "supremely good" (Genesis 1:31)—as if to say, "Now that's *really* good."

If we can imagine a God who delights in creation, dare we imagine a God who delights in *us*? And even more: a God who delights specifically in *you*? Your spouse?

Genesis 2 describes the lush and beautiful garden God gave the man and woman for a home:

> The LORD God planted a garden in Eden in the east and put there the human he had formed. In the fertile land, the LORD God grew every beautiful tree with edible fruit, and also he grew the tree of life in the middle of the garden and the tree of the knowledge of good and evil. –Genesis 2:8-9

Ah, paradise. The good times lasted all of one chapter.

God gave Adam and Eve but one command: don't eat from the tree of knowledge. They disobeyed, and were eventually expelled from the garden before they could take from the tree of life as well.

But that's not all. God's blessing was traded for a curse. The couple's betrayal of God's trust spoiled their once good relationship to the fertile land:

> ...cursed is the fertile land because of you; in pain you will eat from it every day of your life. Weeds and thistles will grow for you, even as you eat the field's plants; by the sweat of your face you will eat bread—until you return to the fertile land, since from it you were taken; you are soil, to the soil you will return. –Genesis 3:17-19

So what does this have to do with peace?

Think of the story so far. The beauty and fruitfulness of the garden reflect the goodness of God's creation, but sin brings a curse. If God were to reverse the curse, if humans were once more blessed for their obedience, what would that blessing look like?

Heaven, we might say. But that begs the question of what we expect heaven to be like. Not winged and chubby cherubs eternally plucking harps, perhaps, but what? Will it be some ethereal, other-worldly experience, or something else?

Consider this downright earthy vision of peace and contentment, given from God in the book of Leviticus. Everything God's people could want is right here:

> If you live according to my rules, keep my commands, and do them, I will give you rain at the proper time, the land will produce its yield, and the trees of the field will produce their fruit. Your threshing season will last until the grape harvest, and the grape harvest will last until planting time. You will eat your fill of food and live securely in your land. I will grant *peace* in the land so that you can lie down without anyone frightening you. I will remove dangerous animals from the land, and no sword will pass through it. … I will walk around among you; I will be your God, and you will be my people. –Leviticus 26:3-6, 12 (emphasis added)

Do you hear it? God's blessing is the mirror image of the curse; the promise brings healing to humanity's *this*-world relationship to the land, the relationship that was broken in Eden.

As in our earlier discussion of peace, there is a negative side to the promise: peace is the absence of fear and danger, enemies and war. But there is also a positive side. Not only will God's people live in security, they will eat their fill, enjoying the continual presence of abundance and fruitfulness.

Peace is also the restoration of fellowship with God. As God once walked in the garden (Genesis 3:8), so now he declares: "I will walk around among you; I will be your God, and you will be my people."

The biblical story, cover to cover, begins with a good creation and ends with a renewed and restored creation. As Andy Crouch has insisted, we must attend to the "bookends"—namely, the first two chapters of the book of Genesis, and the last two chapters of Revelation—or else "miss the whole point of the biblical story."[3]

The story that begins in Eden ends in New Jerusalem, where the promise of God's eternal and direct presence with his people will finally be fulfilled:

> Then I saw a new heaven and a new earth, for the former heaven and the former earth had passed away, and the sea was no more. I saw the holy city, New Jerusalem, coming down out of heaven from God, made ready as a bride beautifully dressed for her husband. I heard a loud voice from the throne say, "Look! God's dwelling is here with humankind. He will dwell with them, and they will be his peoples. God himself will be with them as their God. He will wipe away every tear from their eyes. Death will be no more. There will be no mourning, crying, or pain anymore, for the former things have passed away." –Revelation 21:1-4

And in Revelation 22, the very last chapter of the Bible, we find something familiar, a bookend-to-bookend repetition of a symbol from the garden:

> Then the angel showed me the river of life-giving water, shining like crystal, flowing from the throne of God and the Lamb through the middle of the city's main street. On each side of the river is the tree of life, which produces twelve crops of fruit, bearing its fruit each month. The tree's leaves are for the healing of the nations. There will no longer be any curse. The throne of God and the Lamb will be in it, and his servants will worship him. –Revelation 22:1-3

There it is: the tree of life. The man and woman had been driven out of paradise, to keep them from eating from that tree and becoming immortal in their sin (Genesis 3:22-24). So the story began. But by the end of the story, the curse is abolished, and the tree of life becomes the source of healing that it was always meant to be—that God created it to be.

Creation; the curse of sin; redemption and renewal: this is the story the Bible tells.

From the goodness of creation, through the ongoing curse of sin and rebellion, to redemption, restoration, and renewal: this is the story the Bible tells. This is the framework for its vision of peace, the vision that grounds and gives meaning to our divine vocation as peacemakers.

A biblical understanding of peace is not just the negation of war, sin, or suffering. The English word "peace" translates the Hebrew word "shalom," a concept rich in positive content:

> In the Bible, shalom means universal flourishing, wholeness, and delight—a rich state of affairs in which natural needs are satisfied and natural gifts fruitfully employed, a state of affairs that inspires joyful wonder as its Creator and Savior opens doors and welcomes the creatures in whom he delights. Shalom, in other words, is the way things ought to be.[4]

"The way things ought to be": the way things were created to be, with all the inherent and delight-giving goodness with which they were originally endowed by the Creator.

Jesus says that those who make peace are blessed, "because they will be called God's children" (Matthew 5:9)—they will carry on the legacy of their Father, the God of peace (Romans 15:33). And they will do so because they know themselves to be part of the grand story of God's restoration of shalom to creation.

Now that's *good.*

Those Whom God Has Joined Together

Peacemakers don't just imagine shalom as the end of the story; their kingdom calling is to show that peace is possible in the here and now, even and perhaps especially in their closest relationships. Marriage originally shared in God's good creation, and that goodness was marred and distorted by sin. Can we envision ourselves as part of God's work of renewal?

Whenever I officiate a wedding, I ask the couple if they have a particular passage of Scripture they would like me to include in the sermon. The most popular text by far is Paul's description of love in 1 Corinthians 13.

But running a close second is another text from the creation story in Genesis 2, a text that speaks to the close and mysterious union of husband and wife:

> Then the LORD God said, "It's not good that the human is alone. I will make him a helper that is perfect for him." … So the LORD God put the human into a deep and heavy sleep, and took one of his ribs and closed up the flesh over it. With the rib taken from the human, the LORD God fashioned a woman and brought her to the human being. The human said, "This one finally is bone from my bones and flesh from my flesh. She will be called a woman because from a man she was taken." This is the reason that a man leaves his father and mother and embraces his wife, and they become one flesh. –Genesis 2:18,21-24

We are not told exactly what the "one-flesh" relationship means. There is, of course, a sexual dimension to it, but the context suggests so much more. As David Gushee writes, "Though the human person withers apart from relationship with his Creator, it is not only his Creator he needs."[5] Adam needs a "helper"—not a subordinate, but a companion, a matching half, a true life partner. None of the other creatures will do. But when Eve is fashioned from his own flesh and bone and brought to him, Adam blurts out (I imagine, excitedly), "This is the one! Finally!"

The two become one. The individuals don't cease to exist; one doesn't absorb the other. But something new is created, something more than just the sum of the two: a marriage, a sacred relationship of unity. In the language of the traditional western church wedding, the bride and groom covenant to maintain their commitment to each other and to the relationship through thick and thin, "till death do us part," while the minister intones, "Those whom God hath joined together let no man put asunder."

Suffice it to say, however, that there's an awful lot of parting and sundering going on these days.

In 2014, for example, celebrity couple Gwyneth Paltrow and Chris Martin decided to divorce. Or to be more accurate, they decided to "consciously uncouple," as Paltrow publicly explained on her website:

> It is with hearts full of sadness that we have decided to separate. We have been working hard for well over a year… and we have come to the conclusion that while we love each other very much we will remain separate. We are, however, and always will be a family, and in many ways we are closer than we have ever been. We are parents first and foremost, to two incredibly wonderful children and we ask for their and our space and privacy to be respected at this difficult time. We have always conducted our relationship privately, and we hope that as we consciously uncouple and coparent, we will be able to continue in the same manner.[6]

"Consciously uncouple": the phrase left many scratching their heads. Some dismissed it as vain New Age psychobabble, especially amidst the ever-present rumors of secret skeletons hiding in closets.

But let's be fair. We may have mental images of celebrities blithely and irresponsibly abandoning their marriages at the first sign of unpleasantness, but on the face of it at least, that's not what Paltrow describes. Whatever the nature of the work they've done on their relationship, at least they've done *something*; their decision to separate is not a joyous one; and they are trying to do right by their children by staying involved as parents.

Who knows what the future may bring? But at least what she's described as their goals is more than I could say for some couples.

To be clear: I firmly believe that divorce runs directly counter to God's intention for marriage. But this isn't a simple matter of breaking the rules. It's because in the storyline that begins with creation, runs through sin and brokenness, and ends with full restoration and renewal, divorce should *always* be considered a tragic turn, no matter the circumstances. Just ask people who have been divorced. Many will tell you that even if it was mutually agreed upon (it often isn't) and both believed it to be the right decision, it was nevertheless painful, sometimes excruciatingly so—and often continued to be so for years after.

In a broken world, divorce is inevitable. If Paltrow prefers the language of "conscious uncoupling," it's at least partly because she regards the decision as final and wants to be intentional about avoiding unnecessary pain and acrimony. Frankly, I think that's commendable, as far as it goes.

The problem, though, is that the concept also seeks to remove the tragic element of divorce by telling a different story about marriage.

Below the announcement of her decision, Paltrow posted an explanation of conscious uncoupling written by Habib Sadeghi and Sherry Sami. Here's a short sample from the much longer and more complicated statement:

> To change the concept of divorce, we need to release the belief structures we have around marriage that create rigidity in our thought process. The belief structure is the all-or-nothing idea that when we marry, it's for life. The truth is, the only thing any of us have is today. Beyond that, there are no guarantees. The idea of being married to one person for life is too much pressure for anyone. In fact, it would be interesting to see how much easier couples might commit to each other by thinking of their relationship in terms of daily renewal instead of a lifetime investment.[7]

The authors argue that people live much longer than they used to, and marriage just wasn't built to survive that long a commitment. If it does, great—but no one should expect it. Their recommendation is to dump that outdated idea, and commit for today instead.

Could it be they've been listening to John Lennon?

It's true that there are important and valid reasons to focus on today. To take lifetime commitment for granted as some kind of externally imposed rule, while ignoring the work that needs to be done in the marriage today, is certainly unwise. After all, didn't Jesus himself say, "stop worrying about tomorrow, because tomorrow will worry about itself. Each day has enough trouble of its own" (Matthew 6:34)?

Indeed. But he said this in the context of the command to desire God's kingdom and righteousness above all. We're not to worry about daily necessities like food and clothing: instead, we're asked to trust that God will care for all our needs (Matthew 6:25-33).

God's kingdom has already begun. Jesus invites his followers to take part, to believe that one day sin and suffering will be no more. But meanwhile, there's work to do. Thus, when Jesus teaches his disciples to focus on today, he isn't saying that there's no tomorrow. Quite the contrary: he's saying that today and tomorrow alike are in the hands of a loving heavenly Father. It's *because* tomorrow belongs to God that they can more confidently attend to today.

What Sadeghi and Sami don't seem to consider is the possibility that a commitment "till death do us part" can actually be *empowering* rather than constraining. To put it bluntly, it's hard to commit the time and emotional energy needed to heal marital rifts when you've already got one eye on the door, and keep thinking about how much better things will be once the marriage is dissolved.

Please don't get me wrong. I am *not* saying that there are no circumstances in which, on balance, divorce is the sanest option. Nor am I wagging a big fat finger in the faces of those who have already divorced, condemning them as rule-breakers.

That way of thinking, in fact, is part of the problem that fuels the need for seemingly more neutral and compassionate concepts like conscious uncoupling in the first place. What we suffer throughout the church is not just a crisis of divorce, but a crisis of imagination. We have trouble imagining peace.

Sometimes, in our congregations, we dare not speak openly about divorce. It's just too awkward. We know the statistics: divorce is quite commonplace, even in the church. Many of our brothers and sisters have suffered through it, and are sitting next to us in worship services with their new spouses.

We often think of righteousness in terms of following rules: here are the things Christians can and should do, and here are the things they can't. Divorce, supposedly, is in the latter category. Again, didn't Jesus himself say so (Matthew 5:31-32)? So what do we do with people who are breaking the rules? Tell them to stop? Or just turn a blind eye to it all and not say a word?

Here's an alternative. The kingdom righteousness of which Jesus speaks is not a simple matter of following rules. Think of it this way. Many couples, who in their hearts no longer want their marriage, nevertheless stay together "for the sake of the children," and that may in fact be in the children's best interests. So far, so good. But if their decision is mostly about obeying rules that say, "Don't divorce," and "Don't abandon your kids," then "staying together" may mean little more than continuing to live in the same household while barely tolerating each other's existence.

That's not peace.

The Pharisees represented a complex religious system of rule-based righteousness, and repeatedly criticized Jesus for infractions. But Jesus was not a lawbreaker; he was a Law-fulfiller (Matthew 5:17). He showed the true intent of God's Instruction in the way he lived, and called his disciples to do the same.

It's crucial for peacemakers to understand the difference. It's possible to read Jesus as teaching that the Pharisees were on the right track but didn't go far enough. For example, I can honestly say that as far as the Ten Commandments are concerned, I've never murdered anyone. Nor have I cheated on my wife. But then Jesus says that people who get boiling mad at a brother or sister are guilty of murder in God's eyes, and that anyone who harbors lust is guilty of adultery (Matthew 5:21-30). *Deal with **that**, you Pharisees. You're not as righteous as you thought you were!* Well, then neither am I.

But as Glen Stassen has argued, Jesus' point was not to up the ante on rule-based righteousness, but to encourage "transforming initiatives of peacemaking."[8] For example:

> The truth is that Jesus gave no command not to be angry. What Jesus says here about anger is instead a diagnosis. It is a participle, "being angry"—an ongoing action, continuing in anger; being angry leads to judgment.[9]

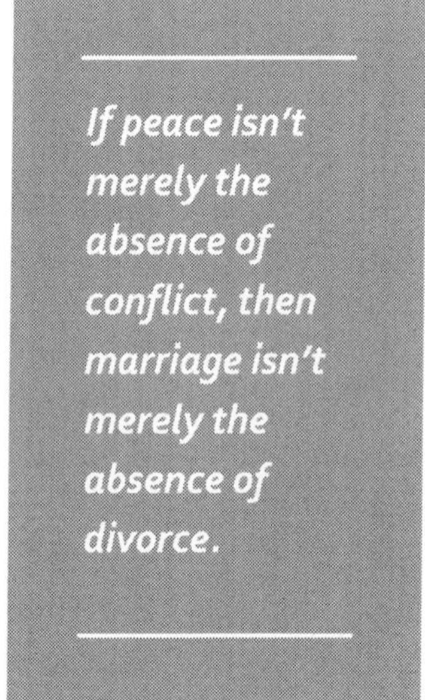
If peace isn't merely the absence of conflict, then marriage isn't merely the absence of divorce.

We can't sit back and congratulate ourselves for not having murdered our spouses. Instead, if we're going to follow Jesus' lead, we must recognize the negative spiral of anger and blame in which we're trapped, and prayerfully take the initiative to pursue reconciliation.

If peace is not merely the absence of conflict, then marriage is not merely the absence of divorce. Instead of telling people what they can't do, what transforming initiatives can we encourage instead, and on the basis of what positive vision? If we're to be peacemakers—active agents of God's shalom—in a world of troubled marriages and conscious uncoupling, we'll need a vision of peace that is capable of capturing and holding our imagination.[10]

Making Peace—Up, Down, and Sideways

John Paul Lederach knows a thing or two about peace. As both a sociologist and a committed Mennonite, he has worked tirelessly for decades in the cause of international peace. He has story after inspiring story to tell of the courageous initiatives taken by people from all walks of life to end conflict and division, even in the most violent and dangerous of situations.

One sheepishly wonders, after reading a few of these hair-raising tales, why we have so much trouble with smaller and pettier conflicts, especially at home.

What is it that enables people to be peacemakers in this way? The common thread, Lederach suggests, is that they all possess a certain kind of moral imagination, a capacity to creatively envision possibilities that others can't yet see. Such imagination allows these people to: (1) see themselves as part of a web of relationships, and to humbly accept their own personal responsibility in the situation; (2) tolerate the complexity and paradox of opposing points of view as they search for deeper truth; (3) create a social environment that is open to trying something new and creative; and (4) take the risks necessary to pursue a lasting peace.[11]

Think for a moment what this might look like in a marriage relationship:

1. Instead of merely blaming each other for being pig-headed or insensitive (insert your favorite insult), we would step back, realize that "it takes two to tango," and wonder about our part in the conflict;
2. Instead of stubbornly insisting that "I'm right, therefore you're wrong," we would allow the possibility that both of us may be right in our own way, and dig deeper to understand how;
3. Instead of automatically pooh-poohing every suggestion for change our spouses might make, we would talk openly and creatively about new ways to think and behave;
4. Instead of continuing to defend ourselves against being hurt again, we would realize that someone has to take the first step, and be willing to take the risk.

Yes, I know: you may have good reason to avoid risk. You've been hurt, possibly even physically or emotionally abused. And well-meaning people may have added insult to injury by minimizing the injustice you've suffered, blaming you for the problem, or telling you that if you would just follow these two or three simple steps, everything would be okay.

Maybe that's why Jesus begins the Beatitudes by saying, "Happy are people who are hopeless, because the kingdom of heaven is theirs" (Matthew 5:3). Even if no one else understands the pain of powerlessness, Jesus does—and *still* bids you to believe that the kingdom is yours, and that you are called to the path of peace.

Lederach is not talking about rules of engagement or principles of conflict resolution, as some uses of the language of peacemaking might suggest.[12] He's talking about imagination, about the kind of vision that makes change possible.

Biblically, what might such a vision entail? We've talked about the bookends of the story—from the first creation to the new creation. It's time to fill in more of the middle.

℘℘

As I write these words, the season of Lent is drawing to a close and Easter approaches. Christians everywhere will be encouraged once again to reflect upon the significance of the crucifixion and resurrection of Jesus.

In some Christian circles, the gospel is spoken of primarily in terms of how it is good news for *me*, personally. Because of my sin, I had no chance at heaven. But thank God for the cross! Jesus died in my place, taking away the penalty for my sins, and now I can go to heaven when I die. Jesus triumphed over death, and therefore, by the grace of God, so will I.

Yes, yes, and yes. But that's not the whole story. The gospel of God's kingdom is not only about the death that Jesus died, but the life that he lived: a life of both humility and power, of love for both his friends and enemies, even for the disenfranchised of polite society.

We are invited into the death of Jesus so that we may also enter his life: not just resurrection as a future event but as a present reality, expressed in the transformed lives of those who live by his Spirit (e.g., Romans 8:5-11).

> *We are invited into the death of Jesus so that we may also enter his life.*

All of this is the work of peace. It begins with the up-down vertical dimension of what God has done to restore a right relationship between us and him. As Paul writes in his letter to the church in Rome:

> God shows his love for us, because while we were still sinners Christ died for us. ... If we were reconciled to God through the death of his Son while we were still enemies, now that we have been reconciled, how much more certain is it that we will be saved by his life? –Romans 5:8,10

God has reconciled us to himself through the cross. Because of this, Paul can confidently declare, "we have peace with God through our Lord Jesus Christ" (Romans 5:1).

But peace has a sideways, horizontal dimension as well: as Christians, we are to be agents of God's reconciling peace in our earthly relationships. Tangible expressions of peace should abound between believers:

> Therefore, as God's choice, holy and loved, put on compassion, kindness, humility, gentleness, and patience. Be tolerant with each other and, if someone has a complaint against anyone, forgive each other. As the Lord forgave you, so also forgive each other. And over all these things put on love, which is the perfect bond of unity. The peace of Christ must control your hearts—a peace into which you were called in one body. –Colossians 3:12-15

Think of your own experiences in local congregations. Then imagine a church family in which all these things were true, or at least represented a shared vision of peace: love, compassion, kindness, humility, gentleness, patience, forgiveness.

Isn't that a church you would join?

Moreover, God's peace, ushered in through the cross, even bridges the frequently unchallenged, seemingly self-evident gulf between believers of different ethnic and cultural backgrounds:

> Christ is our peace. He made both Jews and Gentiles into one group. With his body, he broke down the barrier of hatred that divided us. He canceled the detailed rules of the Law so that he could create one new person out of the two groups, making peace. He reconciled them both as one body to God by the cross, which ended the hostility to God.
>
> –Ephesians 2:14-16

Imagine how Paul's first-century audience might have heard this. The ongoing, confusing struggle between Jewish and Gentile believers casts a long shadow over Paul's letters. He needs these believers not just to change their behavior, but to catch a vision.

So he paints them a rich and complex word picture. Jesus died on the cross, but Paul also says, literally, that through the cross God killed the hatred between us and him. That's the vertical dimension. And Jesus, through his broken body, both breaks down the old wall of hatred and prejudice that separates Jews from Gentiles, and makes these former enemies into one body in him. That's the horizontal dimension.

Up, down, sideways. The vertical movement of peace both empowers and demands the horizontal: what God has done, we must also do.

And that includes in our marriages.

℘ᦓ

Paul doesn't say much about marriage, and what he does say, unfortunately, can easily be taken out of context. That's very much the case with the one passage in which he speaks of both marriage and peace together:

> If a believer has a wife who doesn't believe, and she agrees to live with him, then he shouldn't divorce her. If a woman has a husband who doesn't believe and he agrees to live with her, then she shouldn't divorce him. The husband who doesn't believe belongs to God because of his wife, and the wife who doesn't believe belongs to God because of her husband. Otherwise, your children would be contaminated by the world, but now they are spiritually set apart. But if a spouse who doesn't believe chooses to leave, then let them leave. The brother or sister isn't tied down in these circumstances. God has called you to peace. How do you know as a wife if you will save your husband? Or how do you know as a husband if you will save your wife? –1 Corinthians 7:12-16

Paul's intent is neither to write a treatise on the theology of marriage, nor to create a rule or loophole that says, "If your unbelieving spouse deserts you, then divorce is okay."[13] Instead, he is writing as an absentee pastor trying to teach the way of peace to a contentious congregation.

The church at Corinth was one in which people had experienced the gifts of the Holy Spirit in obvious and remarkable ways. But they were still steeped in prideful and worldly ways of thinking; spiritual experiences tended to divide rather than unite the church.

In that context, marriage and sexuality became issues about which they wrote seeking Paul's counsel. Some Corinthians, for example, seemed convinced that their newfound (and superior!) spirituality demanded that they refrain from sexual relations, even in marriage (1 Corinthians 7:1). Against this, Paul taught that husbands and wives should, in mutual service, meet each other's sexual needs (vss. 2-6).

But here's another situation, one with a more contemporary ring. Think, for example, of the story of Lee and Leslie Strobel.[14] Neither were believers when they first married, and all seemed well. But it wasn't long before Leslie became a Christian. Though she desired desperately for Lee to follow her into the faith, he resisted, and a painful gap opened between them.

Something similar appears to have been happening in Corinth. What to do? To divorce or not to divorce: that is the question. Reading between the lines, given how proud the Corinthians were of their spirituality, we might guess that some new believers were throwing aside their marriages to unbelieving spouses, all in the name of Christ.

Notice Paul's response. He doesn't seem to be just "laying down the law": he explicitly tells them that he's giving them his opinion, rather than a command straight from the lips of Jesus (vs. 12).

But like Jesus, he encourages a transforming initiative: the believing spouses should pursue peace.[15] In this case, it means that believing spouses should demonstrate humility by respecting what the other spouse wants. *Do they want to stay? Then let them stay; don't divorce. Do they want to leave? Then let them leave; don't prevent them.* And though the exact meaning of his words isn't clear, he seems to be giving them a larger vision: *Listen—God still has his eye on your kids, and you really don't know what he might yet do in your marriage.*

All that to say this. In a marriage between believers, everything said about peace in Colossians 3 already applies: the relationship should be one of humility, gentleness, compassion, and the like. But even believers who are married to non-believers are still called to peace: respecting their spouse's wishes, not pridefully abandoning their marriages, and not using their religion as a stick.

℘℘

We worship a God of peace (Romans 15:33). We have been saved by the Prince of Peace (Isaiah 9:6). Through the Holy Spirit, it is peace that binds believers together in unity (Ephesians 4:3).

Is it any wonder that we have been called to make peace in our relationships, in our marriages, to bring into tangible fruition the story of God's ongoing work of peace in which we already stand?

The work takes faith, and faith needs vision. But please note: this doesn't mean that in each and every situation in your marriage there is one specific thing you must do to make peace, and it's your job to find it lest you incur God's displeasure. As one who follows Jesus, you have been invited to participate in a glorious work of God: the work of peace, of restoration, of reconciliation. By God's design, that work must find concrete expression in daily life through the things we do and say as peacemakers.

This may be more art than science. Ron Martoia, for example, uses improvisational theater as a metaphor for how the church enacts the biblical story. It is less an "owner's manual" than a "dramatic script" into which believers immerse themselves.[16] He writes:

> Improvisation is a learned art form. ...It requires immersion in the biblical story so that our improvisation is in continuity with the story told so far. And then it requires a creative and imaginative grappling with the questions of our time, so that the biblical story extends and expands as we model how to live as the people of God in this new time.[17]

So use your imagination. Imagine your marriage as part of God's grand work of peace and renewal. Imagine what God wants to do in your relationship to be able to say, as he did in Genesis, "Now that's good." What will it take for you to do your part? That's one way for you to make peace at home.

❧☙

Questions for discussion and reflection:

1. What do you do when you want to experience "peace"? Go for a walk? Pray? Hide in a closet? Describe both the negative and positive aspects of the experience: what negative things are you

getting away from, and what positive things do you enjoy?

2. Read the creation story in Genesis 1. When God sees that what he has created is "good," can you imagine him actually taking delight in it? Why or why not? Can you imagine God taking delight in you? Your spouse?

3. Discuss the idea of being married for life. Is it an idea that (a) you take for granted without thinking about it, (b) makes you a little nervous, (c) inspires you, or (d) provokes you in some other way? Respond to the quote from Sadeghi and Sami. What is it about the quote, if anything, that seems at least a little bit right to you, and why? What seems wrong?

4. Read again Lederach's four elements of moral imagination and their application to marital conflict. What, out of all that is described there, reminds you of something in your own marriage? Tell a story. If possible, focus on the positive things that you want to see more of in your relationship.

5. Is there anything about your marriage now that you can imagine God looking at and saying, "That's good"? What's your part in it? Your spouse's part? This may point to something one or both of you already do well in your relationship. What can you do to show appreciation to each other for such things, and not take them for granted?

6. Now think of an area of your marriage that needs improvement. Think specifically of what your part would be in moving that part of your marriage toward wholeness. Find the words to translate that into a personal goal: "To be more of a peacemaker in my marriage, I will ____." How will you regularly remind yourself of that goal so that it becomes real to you?

3

EVERY MARRIAGE NEEDS HOPE

In chapter 2, we looked at a biblical vision of peace as God's shalom: the wholeness and flourishing that characterized creation, including the unity of the marriage relationship. As peacemakers, we need to imagine ourselves as part of God's story of restoring wholeness to a creation marred by sin. He has made peace with us. He calls us to make peace with others. But because what we do today is affected by how we see tomorrow, we must discuss how peacemakers need to be people of hope.

ꟸ

Like most people, I love a good story. As a boy, I read comic books, then detective fiction, then science fiction and sword-and-sorcery fantasy novels. When I became a dad, I had the joy of sharing stories with my kids. I made up bedtime stories that would set them to giggling instead of winding down for sleep. For *Winnie-the-Pooh*, I'd imitate the voices from the Disney cartoons. And being overly ambitious, I also tried to invent voices for all the characters in C. S. Lewis' Narnia and J. R. R. Tolkien's Middle-Earth—and frequently lost track of which voice was whose ("No, Daddy, Legolas doesn't talk that way!").

The best stories capture our imaginations, allow us to experience other times and places, even whole worlds. In that regard, *The Lord of the Rings* is still my favorite work of fantasy fiction. Hobbits, elves, and dwarves don't exist, of course, but it doesn't matter. Middle-Earth was very nearly real to me, a place with a rich and complex history, where good and evil struggled for control of lands and hearts alike.

In one of the story's most memorable passages, Frodo the hobbit and his faithful companion Sam, with the untrustworthy creature Gollum as their guide, are making their way secretly into the land of Mordor. They alone are left to carry out a quest to save Middle-Earth: they must find their way to Mount Doom to destroy the magical ring that is the source of the evil sorcerer Sauron's power.

They stop to rest and eat. Exhausted, Frodo complains to Sam that all of Mordor feels oppressive. But he is resigned to finishing the quest. "So our path is laid," he says, and Sam agrees, adding that they might not have come at all if they had known what they were getting themselves into. But, he muses, this seems to be the way adventures often go:

> I used to think that [adventures] were things the wonderful folk of the stories went out and looked for, because they wanted them, because they were exciting... But that's not the way of it with the tales that really mattered, or the ones that stay in the mind. Folk seem to have been just landed in them, usually—their paths were laid that way, as you put it. But I expect they had lots of chances, like us, of turning back, only they didn't. And if they had, we shouldn't know, because they'd have been forgotten. We hear about those as just went on—and not all to a good end, mind you; at least not to what folk inside a story and not outside it call a good end. You know, coming home, and finding things all right, though not quite the same... But those aren't always the best tales to hear, though they may be the best tales to get landed in! I wonder what sort of a tale we've fallen into?[1]

"What sort of a tale have we fallen into?" Sam asks. *How will it end? What will be the result of all our sacrifices?*

That, in essence, is the question of hope.

For the two beleaguered hobbits, hope is not some blind, sunny optimism. With every step, the path becomes harder. Grimly, they realize that there are no provisions left for a return journey. All that is left to them is their mutual loyalty and shared determination to finish what they've started.

And at last, they do. The ring is destroyed in the fires of Mount Doom. Sauron's power is broken; Mordor itself begins to collapse all around them. Frodo, utterly spent, lies down to die. "Hopes fail," he tells Sam. "An end comes. We have only a little time to wait now. We are lost in ruin and downfall, and there is no escape."[2]

But Sam, out of love for his master, refuses to give up. Bit by bit, he coaxes Frodo down the slope of the crumbling mountain. And when at last they can go no further, Sam says bravely, "What a tale we have been in, Mr. Frodo, haven't we? … I wish I could hear it told! … And I wonder how it will go on after our part."

Frodo and Sam, of course, are about to be rescued, but don't know that. As they await their end, their only defense against fear is knowing that they have somehow been part of a tale "that really mattered," a story that will continue after they're gone.

൭൫

I've met many couples over the years who badly needed an infusion of hope. Some lived in quiet desperation that the difficulties they faced would never—*could* never—change. Others had simply resigned themselves to the status quo: *That's the way it is; that's the way it will always be; better just get used to it.*

When circumstances get us down, it's natural to look for something or someone to blame. Sometimes we blame ourselves, but more often, we blame each other. And when we do so, we frequently fall into what psychologists call an *attribution bias*. Whatever *we* may have done wrong was due to situational factors that were outside our control—heck, any reasonable person in that situation would have done the same. But our spouses? They did what they did because of their faulty character: they're mean, or selfish, or controlling, or clingy, or, or, or… the list goes on, *ad nauseam*.

I'm not saying we've just imagined the seemingly mean or selfish things our spouses have done. But as we'll see again in a later chapter, marital therapists warn that "Most of us react more to our interpretation of what was actually said than to what our partner meant and did say."[3]

And while such negative explanations might make us feel more justified for a while, they are in their own way counsels of despair: if the problem really is in our spouse's character, what hope is there for change? That way of thinking can trap us into an endless loop of negativity that will sap our own motivation to seek what's best for our relationship.

As suggested in previous chapters, we need a broader vision, a more comprehensive story that doesn't begin and end with marriage. What sort of a tale have you been "landed in"? And is it one that really matters?

On Love Stories and Soul Mates

We love stories because we *live* stories. And—if it's not too confusing to say it this way!—we live love stories. In other words, part of the story we want to tell about our lives may be a love story.

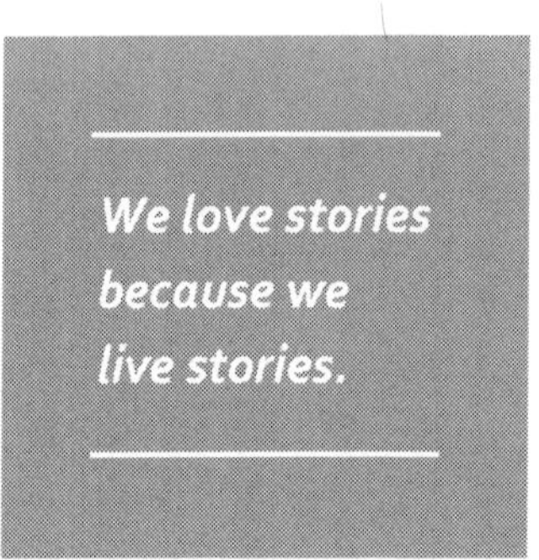
We love stories
because we
live stories.

Here's the well-worn plotline of so many romantic Hollywood tales. Boy meets girl—and sometimes even to their surprise, they fall deeply in love. Through the jealous actions of a party, or a comic misunderstanding, boy loses girl, and they struggle to find one another again. The climax of the story is their happy reunion, and as the credits roll, we're meant to believe that they'll live happily ever after.

Maybe we don't really believe that love and romance happen this way in real life. But it's hard to deny the pull such stories have on our imaginations.

For example: the plot of 1993's *Sleepless in Seattle* piggybacked on the classic 1957 tear-jerker, *An Affair to Remember,* starring Cary Grant and Deborah Kerr. In *Sleepless*, Annie (Meg Ryan), who is already engaged to boring but reliable Walter (Bill Pullman), inexplicably falls in love with a widower named Sam (Tom Hanks) whom she merely hears on a radio talk show.

Annie and her friend Becky (Rosie O'Donnell) have watched *Affair* so often that they've memorized the dialogue. They believe in the story's lesson of romantic destiny. Annie, seized by the idea that she and Sam are fated to be together, secretly begins stalking him. She even breaks off her engagement with Walter, on the mere chance of meeting Sam atop the Empire State Building, the scene of a tragically failed rendezvous in *Affair*.

The film, of course, has a happy ending, though Sam and Annie don't actually meet until the final scene. But the script raises an important moral issue, nicely voiced by Becky, who wryly tells Annie, "You don't want to be in love. You want to be in love *in a movie*."

What about us? Are the movies just a pleasant diversion, or do they somehow both reflect and shape our expectations of romance?

In the months after the movie's release, officials at the Empire State Building were inundated with phone calls. Some callers wanted to know if they were going to make the big red heart light up again on the side of the building for Valentine's Day, not realizing that this was just a special effect created for the movie. Others called hoping to arrange marriage proposals on the observation deck.[4]

That should tell us something about the power of film to shape our love stories. Through words and images, stories and metaphors, popular culture influences our expectations of romance and marriage. Back in the 1990s, for example, it became popular to talk about wanting to find one's "soul mate."

As explained by the spiritual writer Thomas Moore in a 1994 bestseller, a soul mate

> is someone to whom we feel profoundly connected, as though the communicating and communing that take place between us were not the product of intentional efforts, but rather a divine grace. This kind of relationship is so important to the soul that many have said there is nothing more precious in life.[5]

But how popular was the idea? How many people actually believed they had soul mates, and expected to find them?

Apparently, quite a few. In 2001, researchers at the National Marriage Project surveyed over 1,000 people in their twenties, asking just such questions. Of the over 600 never-married singles in the group that responded,

- 94% agreed with the statement "when you marry you want your spouse to be your soul mate, first and foremost";
- 88% agreed that their soul mate was "waiting for [them] somewhere out there";
- 87% expected they would actually find their soul mates.[6]

I don't know what percentage of people still think this way. But as the authors of a recent book still claim:

> Millions of us dream of experiencing a deeply connected relationship that grows richer and more intimate with time. We believe that our soulmates—with whom we're emotionally, physically, and spiritually in sync—are out there somewhere, if only we know how to find them.[7]

"Millions." Exaggerated rhetoric? Perhaps. Let's just say that the soul mate idea isn't gone quite yet.

Is that such a bad thing? What's wrong with wanting a deep emotional connection with our spouses? Knowing what each other is thinking or feeling, even finishing each other's sentences? Isn't that the kind of thing that the "one flesh" relationship of the creation story is all about?

There's absolutely nothing wrong with wanting more emotional intimacy in your marriage. The question is what place such intimacy has in your life story. As we saw in chapter 1, happiness is not something you aim at directly; it's a by-product of "getting the conditions right." It's not a matter of finding the right person, but becoming the right person yourself.

Here's what I worry about. Many Christians seem to buy into a somewhat sanctified version of the soul mate idea (doesn't the word "soul" sound appropriately spiritual?). That special someone isn't just "out there somewhere"—God, as the belief goes, has already picked out just the right person for you. It's only a matter of time and diligent prayer before you discover who it is.

Of course, sometimes that way of thinking seems to "work": by waiting and praying for God to show them whom they should marry, people land the spouse of their dreams. And God, of course, can do whatever he chooses.

I just don't see a compelling biblical basis for believing that this is the way marriage is supposed to be.

☙❧

Certainly, Scripture has its romantic love stories. Take the tale of Isaac and Rebekah (Genesis 24). Abraham, Isaac's father, is getting older. His wife Sarah has died, he knows his own time is near, and he wants his affairs to be in order. He doesn't want his son to marry a foreigner, so he commissions his oldest and most trusted servant to go back to their homeland and find Isaac a wife. The servant takes a solemn vow and sets out on the journey.

But what will he do when he gets there? How will he know whom to choose? He does what so many of us have done: he prays for a sign from God. And God, apparently, grants the sign.

Eventually, the beautiful Rebekah is on her way back to Abraham's household, with her father and brother's blessing. She and Isaac see each other from a distance; I almost imagine them running to each other's arms in slow motion. And the end of the story rivals anything from Hollywood: "He married Rebekah and loved her. So Isaac found comfort after his mother's death" (Genesis 24:67). Cue orchestra; roll credits.

But it's *not* the end of the story.

At the beginning of what seems like a romantic tale, Rebekah is an answer to prayer. Two chapters later, however, a fearful Isaac, to save his own skin, lies to the Philistines and puts his wife at risk of sexual violation. And later, after the twins Jacob and Esau are born, the parents play favorites with the children. Eventually, when the boys have grown up a bit and Isaac is an old man, Rebekah connives with Jacob to steal Isaac's blessing from Esau, taking advantage of her husband's failing eyesight and disguising Jacob as his firstborn brother (Genesis 27).

Need I say it? These people don't exactly have a model marriage, and could probably use some serious family therapy. As David and Diana Garland have written:

> What kind of mother feeds the rivalry between her sons, planting ideas in the mind of one of how to steal blessing from the other? There was no trust here, no safety that home is a place where others care for one's well-being. ...It was probably not the first time that she had used the children as pawns in the marital relationship.[8]

And that's just one generation of the family. Even more shenanigans show up later in the relationships between Jacob and his wives, between Jacob and his sons, between Jacob's sons... How is it that these people don't just get kicked out of the Bible for bad behavior?

The tale of Isaac and Rebekah, it turns out, is not about love and romance. It is but a chapter in a much larger narrative: the story of a covenant-keeping God who faithfully blesses his people even when they've done nothing to deserve it. Old Testament scholar Walter Brueggemann puts it this way:

> In every generation, the transmission of the blessing is not only problematic, but laden with mystery. ...[T]he blessing is given in odd ways. We may nonetheless celebrate that the blessing did survive, willy-nilly, into the next generation, even if carried by characters whom the family storyteller regards as unlikely or inappropriate.[9]

How unromantic, even unheroic, from a human point of view. At its core, the story is not about two people finding, choosing, and loving each other; it's about a God who finds and chooses and loves and blesses—tenaciously, mysteriously, almost irrationally. It's not about Isaac and Rebekah's commitment and loyalty to each other, but God's commitment and loyalty to them and to his promise.

❧☙

The Christian version of the soul mate idea can leave people wondering, "Who is the person God has in store for me? What do I have to do for God to show me who it is?" The uncertain and open-ended search can be an anxious one. As a young woman, for example, Leslie Ludy thought that faithfully abstaining from sex before marriage would convince God to send her Mr. Right. But the men she dated had other intentions, and she had to endure the painful breakup of one relationship after another. She writes:

> This was the constant pattern of my love life. Each fling ended with heartbreak and shattered emotions. ...I cried out to God, "Why is this happening to me? I am living a moral life, following Your commands, yet I am miserable! Why aren't You blessing this area of my life? I'm still following the Christian rules—but I'm so unhappy."[10]

The lesson she would finally learn required a fundamental shift of her life perspective and priorities: "I learned to lean on my relationship with Christ for my hope, joy, and security, rather than trying to find those things in a romantic relationship."[11] In a sense, she swapped out storylines. In place of a dominant theme of finding and marrying that special someone (with God's help, of course!), her story became more about growing in relationship to Jesus and the kingdom he proclaimed and embodied.

This isn't just about dating, of course, but marriage. Even if you believe you've found The One, sooner or later something will happen to cool the first flush of optimism. What then? Is there room in the soul mate way of thinking for spouses to recognize that they're both flawed human beings? Or will they just become disillusioned, and be tempted to set the marriage aside and start the search all over again?

Please hear me: I am *not* saying that every divorce can be chalked up to one or both spouses' unrealistic expectations of wedded bliss. I *am* saying, however, that if Christian couples are to maintain hope in the face of difficult marital circumstances, they're going to need something more durable than the romantic tales popular culture provides.

Perhaps that's why, on her first anniversary, newlywed Hannah Wegmann posted a blog entry entitled, "My Husband is Not My Soul Mate." Before marriage, she believed fervently in the Christian romantic ideal that God would someday bring her the husband he had already picked out. When her father, a theologian and Bible scholar, dared to suggest that the Bible didn't promise her a husband, she argued back, quoting Jeremiah 29:11 ("I know the plans I have in mind for you…"). Dad corrected her for taking the verse horribly out of context, then gave her this bit of wisdom:

> There is no biblical basis to indicate that God has one soul mate for you to find and marry. You could have a great marriage with any number of compatible people. There is no ONE PERSON for you.[12]

That doesn't mean that it makes no difference whom you marry. It does mean, however, that courtship and marriage are not a game of *Let's Make a Deal,* in which God has hidden the big prize behind a door, and you have to make the right choice or go home a loser.

God our Father wants the best for his children. But as any parent can tell you, a child's definition of "best" may not be the same as Mom and Dad's.

Living the Right Story

As mentioned earlier, we love stories because we live stories. There are smaller, episodic ones: "Hi, honey—you'll never believe what happened to me today." There are larger stories we tell to make sense of today in light of yesterday: "Well, when I was your age…"

And there are still larger stories that we use to make sense of life itself. My personal story, in which I am the main character, is part of a larger family drama in which others take center stage. My family, in turn, is part of a larger movement of history, of events and ideas that cross time and cultures.

Think, for example, of all the things your parents could or should have done differently in bringing you up. Given the attribution bias mentioned earlier, it's easy to carry a lingering resentment that says, "They should have known better." Even as adults, we may still see our parents through the eyes of who we were as children. No matter how old we get, to us, they're still larger than life.

But then we hear *their* stories: the emotional struggles of the families they grew up in; the hardships they endured as immigrants; the challenges they had to overcome at the hands of abusive bosses. Knowing these things may not excuse all bad behavior, but it puts matters in a different light. Suddenly, we're less sure of the character judgments we've so routinely made. It begins to dawn on us that they're just fallible human beings like us, and maybe, just maybe, there's actually something there to appreciate or even admire.

We'll have a closer look at these ideas in the upcoming chapters on compassion. For now, the point is this: when it comes to hope, it matters what story we tell.

Think back to Hannah Wegmann's story above. I can't begin to count how many times I've heard people use Jeremiah 29:11 the way she did with her father. Perhaps someone has offered them to you as personal words of encouragement, or you've heard them used that way in a sermon. And the words are indeed hopeful:

> I know the plans I have in mind for you, declares the LORD; they are plans for peace, not disaster, to give you a future filled with hope. When you call me and come and pray to me, I will listen to you. When you search for me, yes, search for me with all your heart, you will find me.

But in context, the message is quite different than the one we normally hear or want to hear. Through the prophet Jeremiah, God is telling his people living in exile in Babylon, "I'm the one who carried you into exile. You're going to be there for a while; don't believe anyone who tells you differently. Settle down; build houses, have families. Yes, I'll bring you back to Jerusalem. But you're going to have to wait seventy years first" (Jeremiah 29:4-14).

Wait seventy years for God to keep a promise? Right. We're lucky if our patience holds out for seventy days.

We go to the Bible for words of hope, and rightly so. But the problem is this: when God says, "I know the plans I have for you, plans for peace and a future filled with hope," what we hear is often closer to, "Just be patient and faithful, and God will give you what you want." Truth be told, we're less interested in fitting into God's plans than fitting God into ours. We're less interested in his story of peace than we are in getting the things we think will satisfy our heart's desires.

Here's another example. You're having a tough time; you're uncertain about the future. You ask a friend to pray for you, and of course, she readily agrees. But she also wants to give you a word of encouragement, so she quotes Romans 8:28—"We know that God works all things together for good for the ones who love God, for those who are called according to his purpose."

How often have you had that verse quoted to you? How often have you quoted it to someone else? Many Christians use it the same way they use the verse from Jeremiah (sometimes in the same sermon). It's a more pious way of saying, "Look, you're a Christian, right? That automatically means you love God. So don't worry. You'll see: everything's going to work out fine."

Is that what Paul is saying? Not really. Listen to the way he talks about hope in the preceding verses:

> I believe that the present suffering is nothing compared to the coming glory that is going to be revealed to us. The whole creation waits breathless with anticipation for the revelation of God's sons and daughters. Creation was subjected to frustration, not by its own choice—it was the choice of the one who subjected it—but in the hope that the creation itself will be set free from slavery to decay and brought into the glorious freedom of God's children. We know that the whole creation is groaning together and suffering labor pains up until now. And it's not only the creation. We ourselves who have the Spirit as the first crop of the harvest also groan inside as we wait to be adopted and for our bodies to be set free. We were saved in hope. If we see what we hope for, that isn't hope. Who hopes for what they already see? But if we hope for what we don't see, we wait for it with patience.
>
> –Romans 8:18-25

This is essentially the story of shalom we outlined in chapter 2. All of creation is groaning and suffering because of sin, and we suffer right along with it. But it's not hopeless suffering. A woman in labor suffers (and here again we might hear an echo of the curse in Genesis 3:16)—but also looks forward in anticipation to what is about to be born, knowing that in the joy of that new birth the former groaning will fade away to a dim memory.

For us as Christians, hope and patience come together when we get the story straight. We may groan and suffer in the present, but the Holy Spirit in us confirms that we have a glorious future. Not a future that nestles neatly into *our* plans, but one that bursts the bonds of our earthbound imaginations. Creation suffers and waits: for what? For God to come at last and say to us, "You, you, and you—you are my adopted children." For God to set our bodies free from death and decay. That is the hope that helps us endure:

> On account of his vast mercy, he has given us new birth. You have been born anew into a living hope through the resurrection of Jesus Christ from the dead. You have a pure and enduring inheritance that cannot perish—an inheritance that is presently kept safe in heaven for you. Through his faithfulness, you are guarded by God's power so that you can receive the salvation he is ready to reveal in the last time. You now rejoice in this hope, even if it's necessary for you to be distressed for a short time by various trials. –1 Peter 1:3-6

It is by faith that we believe the story and understand ourselves to be part of it. And it is in hope that we take hold of and live toward its promises.[13] Think of the great roll call of the heroes and heroines of faith in Hebrews 11: Noah, Abraham, Sarah, Moses, and others. The author lauds them for their forward-looking obedience.

- Noah responded in faith "when he was warned about events he hadn't seen yet" (vs. 7).
- Abraham faithfully obeyed God and left his homeland "without knowing where he was going" (vs. 8).
- Sarah, though long past childbearing age, "believed that he who promised was faithful" (vs. 11).
- Moses endured the rigors of God's call upon his life because "he was looking forward to the reward…as if he could see what is invisible" (vss. 26-27).

And yet with all of that, the author also states solemnly:

> All of these people died in faith without receiving the promises, but they saw the promises from a distance and

> welcomed them. They confessed that they were strangers and immigrants on earth. People who say this kind of thing make it clear that they are looking for a homeland. If they had been thinking about the country that they had left, they would have had the opportunity to return to it. But at this point in time, they are longing for a better country, that is, a heavenly one. Therefore, God isn't ashamed to be called their God—he has prepared a city for them. –Hebrews 11:13-16

The text doesn't say that they never complained, never doubted, never cried out to God for an explanation of why things were taking so long. But it does say that they kept going—because they believed, because they had faith, because they had hope in a promised future they couldn't yet see with crystal clarity. And why?

Because of the faithfulness of the one who made the promise.

☙❧

Perhaps you've heard some version of the following story. Once upon a time, a traveler came upon three men at a building site who were laboring with great blocks of stone. He asked the first man, "What are you doing?"

The man barely looked up from his work. "Isn't it obvious?" he replied. "We have to move these stones wherever we're told. It's backbreaking work, but it's all I can get."

The traveler went to the second man and asked the same question. "We're building a wall," he replied. "That's all I know."

But the third man, when asked the question, wiped the sweat from his brow and smiled warmly. "What are we doing?" he replied. "We're building a great cathedral to the glory of God."

A little perspective goes a long way.

In one of my favorite quotes about Christian hope, N. T. Wright helps us understand how the future we imagine, the story we live, can encourage us to persevere in the kingdom-oriented work of peacemaking. "What's the point?" we might ask when the going gets tough, or when we don't get immediate results. This is the point:

> You are not oiling the wheels of a machine that's about to roll over a cliff. You are not restoring a great painting that's shortly going to be thrown on the fire. You are not planting roses in a garden that's about to be dug up for a building site. You are...accomplishing something that will become in due course part of God's new world. Every act of love, gratitude, and kindness...every prayer, all Spirit-led teaching, every deed that spreads the gospel, builds up the church, embraces and embodies holiness rather than corruption, and makes the name of Jesus honored in the world—all of this will find its way, through the resurrecting power of God, into the new creation that God will one day make. ...[W]hat we do in Christ and by the Spirit in the present is not wasted. It will last all the way into God's new world. In fact, it will be enhanced there.[14]

Wright admits that he can't give detailed blueprints of how all of this will look, nor can anyone else. But think back to our mythical bricklayers. We can learn new ways of thinking and behaving in our marriages, but take the attitude of the first man: "I hate doing this, but I guess I have no choice." Likewise, we can take the attitude of the second man: "I suppose there's more to it, but I'm just following instructions."

Or—we can give ourselves more enthusiastically to the task because we can imagine the contribution we are making to something of lasting value, beauty, and holiness, to something that not only witnesses to the possibility of newness in the present, but may even somehow become part of God's renewed creation in the future.

Every marriage needs this kind of hope. Not because every marriage is hopeless, but because the future we envision shapes how we think about life and respond to others in the present.

As we saw in chapter 1, in the Beatitudes, Jesus declares that the kingdom is a present-tense reality that belongs to the hopeless and harassed (Matthew 5:3,10). He also promises future-tense blessings: the blessed will be comforted, will inherit the earth, will receive the fullness of God's mercy.

Christian hope, in essence, resides in the space between "theirs is" and "they will." God's reign of peace has begun, and we are its ambassadors. But the work can be difficult and demanding. If we are going to be peacemakers in our homes, if we are going to persevere in the virtues of humility and compassion, we will need a robust and proper vision of peace to give us hope.

And we will need something else, something that tends to get overlooked in our individualistic ways of approaching the spiritual life: a community of like-minded people who encourage hopeful rather than hopeless ways of thinking and being.

Hope-full Communities

Shane Lopez, a senior scientist at Gallup and a foremost authority on the psychology of hope, tells the inspiring story of Andrew DeVries, a tall and athletic 55-year-old who in 2002 attended a tryout for the Michigan Senior Olympics volleyball team. He impressed the coach, John Wilder. But soon after the tryout, Andy was involved in a motorcycle accident. Surgeons tried to save his crushed leg, but eventually decided to amputate, even drawing a permanent-ink line on his thigh to show Andy where they would cut. The future seemed bleak.

But young Sarah Scholl, a physician's assistant attending Andy, had other ideas. Knowing his fondness for golf, she asked what seemed to Andy a strangely inappropriate question at the time: "What kind of golf ball do you play?"

"Titleist ProV1," he answered, confused.

The next day, he found a pack of Titleist balls in his room.

Sarah was sending him a message. *Imagine standing on the green again. You have a future. Don't give up hope, not now, not yet.*

Finding some much needed blood flow in the injured leg, the surgeons changed their minds about amputation. Eventually, Andy was assigned to rehab. On the day of his transfer, Sarah asked him for a special favor. Her father had died when she was younger; would Andy please be the one to give her away at her wedding? Not that she was actually engaged, nor even had a boyfriend. But she believed in her own future, and wanted Andy to be part of it.

Later, in rehab, Andy received a surprise phone call from John Wilder, congratulating him on making the volleyball team. There was only one condition: he had to get better. He had to be able to stand.

That vision was all the motivation he needed. Seven months later, Andy stood on that volleyball court. His contribution was limited, but the team eventually won the gold.

And seven *years* later, Andy received an email from Sarah. She had a boyfriend—a fiancé, actually. Andy flew to Portland to keep his promise, and joyfully walked Sarah down the aisle.

Here's Lopez's take on the story:

> If we have a vision and plan for the future, we can't help but be pulled forward by life, even when our present betrays us. We start to create a narrative about a future self that competes with the old stories about ourselves. As we fill in more details and take small steps in our future direction, our energy is freed up. When we're excited about "what's next," we invest more in our daily life, and we can see beyond current challenges.[15]

I agree with everything Lopez says here. We can become overly preoccupied with the negative emotions and experiences of yesterday and today, and anticipate a dreary tomorrow of more-of-the-same. Without hope, our story becomes constricted, and there seems to be little point in trying to change the present.

When I first read Andy's story, however, I was dismayed by what Lopez *didn't* say. Yes, we need to imagine a future that pulls us positively forward, that breaks the shackles of the present.

But the more salient point of the story, to me, is that *we can't do this alone*. More often that we would like to admit, we need our own

Sarah Scholl or John Wilder to love us, to lend us their hopeful vision, and to hold us accountable to it.

We need a community of hope.

We need, in short, a community of hope, people who can speak hope into our lives and help us remember the biblical hope we share.

Years ago, I was chatting sympathetically with a friend whose husband had left her for another woman. She felt, of course, deeply betrayed. She had to struggle not only with her own emotions, but those of her children, not to mention the other practical demands of raising them on her own. Despite her anguish, however, she believed that God wanted her to pray for the healing and reconciliation of the relationship.

Her friends at church, however, were not supportive of the idea. "He's a jerk," they insisted. "Just forget about him and move on with your life." Their intentions were good; they could see how much she was suffering, and wanted to help. In their minds, there was no hope for the relationship, and believed that continuing to cling to such an unrealistic vision of the future would only prolong the pain.

Who's right? Based on your own experience, you may have a strong opinion about that, in one direction or the other.

In truth, though, none of us can know the outcome of such a situation for certain. The husband may come home, or he may not. And merely coming back, of course, is no guarantee of the quality of the relationship, or of his future fidelity.

What caused me to grieve for my friend, however, was the loss piled on top of loss, the insult added to injury. Her friends may have been right to believe that the marriage was over because the husband wouldn't be back. But in their attempt to speed healing, they may not have realized how their pessimism was stealing much-needed hope and leaving nothing but depression and despair in its wake.

Nor would false optimism help. I'd be equally aghast if her friends had trotted out Jeremiah 29:11 and Romans 8:28 and told her to cheer up.

No—what we need is a community of people who understand and mourn the depth of human sin and brokenness, and yet still believe that God's kingdom is afoot, still believe in a heavenly hope that gives us a reason to pursue righteousness in the present. We need people who will give us a safe and welcoming space to tell our tales of grief and suffering, while gently reminding us at the proper time that we are all part of a much larger story of God's peace.

Could such conversations really make a difference?

Yes. Perhaps a bigger difference than you might imagine.

At some point in your life, you've probably experienced the "small world" phenomenon. Perhaps you're sitting on a plane, and strike up a conversation with the person in the seat next to you, a total stranger. After a few minutes, you discover a connection: you have a mutual friend, or went to the same school, or had the same pastor, and so on. Researchers have demonstrated the well-known principle of "six degrees of separation": given the size and overlap of our social networks, any person on the planet can be connected in this way to any other person in six or fewer steps.

Of course, someone separated from us by a full six degrees isn't likely to have much influence on our daily lives, or vice versa. But as in the classic Christmas movie, *It's a Wonderful Life*, you might be surprised to realize just how many people your life does touch.

As social researchers Nicholas Christakis and James Fowler have written:

> Our own research has shown that the spread of influence in social networks obeys what we call the Three Degrees of Influence Rule. Everything we do or say tends to ripple through our network, having an impact on our friends (one degree), our friends' friends (two degrees), and even our friends' friends' friends (three degrees).[16]

Think about it. If Christakis and Fowler are right, and everyone in the world had only ten friends, then everything you say or do will impact a thousand lives, in unseen and unacknowledged ways.

Fifteen friends? Over 3,000. Twenty? Now you're impacting 8,000 people, the vast majority of whom you will never meet. What will you do with that kind of influence?

Build for the future of God's kingdom by being a person who spreads hope instead of apathy or despair.

Because we weren't meant to be peacemakers alone.

☙❧

Questions for discussion and reflection:

1. Think back to a favorite story. It can be fiction or non-fiction: movies, books, even family stories are all fair game. The only requirement, in the words of Sam the hobbit, is that the story be one that "really matters" to you, one that has personally inspired you in some way. Summarize the basic plot and say what it is about the story or particular characters that is meaningful to you. Is there something in the story—a wish fulfilled, a goal achieved, a dream come true—with which you identify?

2. Movie discussion: Watch both *An Affair to Remember* and *Sleepless in Seattle*. Talk about your responses to both movies. What, if anything, about each film did you find moving? If Annie were your sister, what would you say to her? Then watch the 1953 classic *Roman Holiday* (Audrey Hepburn's first starring role), and Disney's 2013 animated feature *Frozen*. Compare/contrast the messages about love in all four films, and discuss why these differing messages might be important to you as a Christian.

3. Do you believe (or have you believed) in the Christian version of the soul mate idea, or something similar? How has this affected

the expectations you have for marriage? Do you agree with what Hannah Wegmann's father told her? Why or why not?

4. Read Jeremiah 29:11 and Romans 8:28 out loud, from whatever translation is most familiar to you. Have those verses ever been quoted to you as words of encouragement, or have you used them that way yourself? What was meant? What, if anything, would you say differently now?

5. Discuss the parable of the traveler and the three builders, and the comments on the following page. Which of the three attitudes comes closest to describing the way you feel right now about working on your marital relationship? Which of the three is the one you would *want* to describe your attitude, and why?

6. Discuss your reactions to the story of Andy DeVries. Like Sarah Scholl or John Wilder, who has spoken hope into your life when you needed it? Tell the story. Then consider: for whom could you do the same, and what vision of the future would you give them?

4

HUNGERING FOR THE RIGHT THINGS

In previous chapters, we looked at true happiness, or what the Bible calls "blessing," as a by-product of seeking God's kingdom. We are part of a bigger story of what God is doing to restore peace to creation, and therein lies our hope. A marriage is therefore blessed when the spouses actively pursue peace in their relationship. There's nothing wrong with wanting a little romance or desiring the other benefits of a happy marriage. But from a Christian perspective, these are not the primary goal. We may need, therefore, to reconsider our priorities. Do we really want what God wants?

ꟸꟸ

Back in the first chapter, I asked you to think honestly about all the different ways you might complete the sentence, "If only _____, then I would be happy." Many people would write material things in the blank: a new car, or a bigger house. Some would want a change of circumstance, like a job with better hours or higher pay.

And some, of course, would wish to see real changes in their relationships, particularly in their marriages.

People's reasons for wanting these things vary tremendously, and none of these desires is wrong in itself. But as we've seen, mere changes in circumstance won't do much for our happiness, long term. That's important to know, because our desires are easily manipulated by people who have something to sell.

Take appetite—actual bodily cravings for food and drink—as an example. Store displays and advertising campaigns advise us to "Go anywhere but hungry" and "Obey your thirst." Restaurant commercials show attractive people cheerfully enjoying the latest menu additions. To appease their children, parents take them to McDonalds and buy them—what else?—Happy Meals.

Sadly, when it comes to fast food, the burger you get in the store never looks quite as appetizing as the one on your TV screen. The image is specifically created to stimulate desire, but the reality behind it can be quite different. Years ago, a student of mine told me she had been in a commercial for a national burger chain. In the final scene of the 30-second spot, she and another actor had to sit side by side chewing their burgers with rapturous expressions on their faces. The truth? The meat had been sprayed with extra grease to make the burgers look juicier. When the director yelled "Cut!" each actor spat the cold, congealing mouthful into a bucket.

Yum.

Advertisers know how to manipulate what may begin as a legitimate desire or need. We may be blissfully unaware, but there is a whole science of buying behavior,[1] and the manipulation starts early. Beginning in the 1980s, advertisers, realizing the influence children had on their parents' purchases, began marketing to them directly. The goal was to "get kids to nag their parents and nag them well" about everything from minivans to breakfast cereal.[2]

For example, have you ever noticed how the characters on adults' cereal boxes tend to look straight ahead, while the ones on children's cereal boxes look slightly downward? It helps Cap'n Crunch and the Trix Rabbit to make eye contact with your little ones. And yes, it works: the research demonstrates that such eye contact increases feelings of trust and connection with a brand.[3]

Even among adults.

Again, there is nothing inherently wrong with having wants, desires, and appetites. But if we intend to be peacemakers, we'd be wise to be more aware of the desires that motivate us. When Jesus commanded his disciples to seek the kingdom, he said it as an alternative to worrying about food, drink, and clothing (Matthew 6:25-34). These are, of course, legitimate universal needs. But I wonder: in today's world, would Jesus also have needed to say something about the things we *think* we need after watching an hour of the Home Shopping Network?

Furthermore, the desires we take for granted may have serious relational consequences, as James suggests:

> What is the source of conflict among you? What is the source of your disputes? Don't they come from your cravings that are at war in your own lives? You long for something you don't have, so you commit murder. You are jealous for something you can't get, so you struggle and fight. You don't have because you don't ask. You ask and don't have because you ask with evil intentions, to waste it on your own cravings. –James 4:1-3

Bible scholars disagree whether James literally meant "murder."[4] We don't have to suppose, however, that some Christians were so envious of each other that their quarrels became lethal. It's enough to note that serious struggles between believers can arise from misdirected desire. James suggests that even our prayer lives may be affected: we either fail to go to God in prayer at all, or else approach him selfishly as if he existed only to give us what we want.

James, of course, is talking about the church, but the same principle applies to other relationships—like marriage. This is particularly the case if we think of desire in broad terms: not just bodily pleasures or materialistic longings, but again, anything we seek in the moment that we think will make us happy.

Spouses fight over a number of things—most predictably, money and children.[5] For example, when I work with premarital couples, I have them discuss how they intend to pool their resources after the wedding.[6] To some extent, it's a matter of nailing down practical decisions like whether to have joint or individual bank accounts, how much to save, and so on. But what couples sometimes discover is that money *means* different things to them.

Take Gene and Janna. For Janna, the bride-to-be, money is a symbol of security, a much-needed hedge against the kind of family disasters she experienced in childhood. Her father was irresponsible with money, spending recklessly, getting the family kicked out of their apartment when they couldn't pay the rent. Janna's mother, stretched to her emotional limit by having to work, raise kids, and keep the family from financial ruin, drilled an anxious need for thrift into her daughter's head.

For the groom, Gene, however, money represented freedom. His parents, who had immigrated to the United States, had also preached the virtues of thrift. It was their determination and sheer hard work that saw them through the early days of poverty. Their family business was successful, and Gene grew up in comfort and financial security. But he could never quite understand why they continued to insist on their penny-pinching ways, when they could easily afford a better lifestyle.

Gene knows that he's not financially irresponsible. He's learned enough from his parents to not just throw money away on frivolous purchases. But he wants the freedom to buy nice things—including gifts for Janna. It frustrates him when she's ambivalent about his gifts. But from her side, it's hard not to feel just a little bit panicky when Gene spends money too spontaneously. And the more he tries to talk her out of it, the less secure she feels.

Janna imagines things being one way, in terms of how she would prefer the next chapter of her life story to go: she will marry someone who will never give her cause to worry about their financial future. Gene doesn't disagree with that, but imagines something a little different: he will marry someone who will appreciate his generosity, who will love him for his thoughtfulness.

Earlier, I suggested that our hopes for marriage may be shaped by the romantic ideals of our culture. Maybe that sounds a little too abstract: you don't *really* think of each other in fairy-tale terms.

As Robert Sternberg has suggested, however, "We come to relationships with many preconceived ideas," including implicit stories and images of what love and marriage *should* be.[7] Without even consciously recognizing it, part of us may hope to find someone who will play a complementary role in our ideal of married life. Those expectations aren't necessarily wrong or bad, and sometimes it all works out.

But again, there's the image, and there's reality. Often, the gap between the ideal of who we *thought* we were marrying and the reality of the person we actually married becomes the source of disillusionment and conflict.

We all have expectations that we bring to marriage, our image of what marriage should be. It can begin with the dream of a perfect wedding, a vision encouraged by an enormous bridal industry. One pastor, in fact, told me of a wedding in which all the bridesmaids and groomsmen seemed unusually good-looking. As he eventually found out, they were all models, hired for the event to make for more impressive looking wedding pictures.

After the wedding, it's time to get down to the business of being married well to a real person who will sometimes let us down.

Truly, I can't even tell you the last time my wife and I looked at *our* wedding album. It's there for the sake of posterity, and maybe the occasional trip down memory lane. But whatever Kodak moments couples might generate (or stage!), *after* the wedding, it's time to get down to the business of being married well to a real person whom we love, but who will also let us down or hurt us.

So here's the question: why are you reading this book? Why read about marriage and peacemaking? What do you hope to accomplish by it? The Bible sometimes speaks of our needs and desires using the language of hunger and thirst. And Jesus just might have something to say about that.

Hunger Pangs

Hunger is a global problem. As human beings, we need to eat to survive. But by some estimates, over 800 million people don't have enough food.[8] That's about one-eighth of the world's population. Nearly as many are without access to safe drinking water, leaving thousands of children to die of water-borne illnesses.[9]

Hunger and thirst have always been problems for the poorest of the world's societies. That's why the good news of God's kingdom is often framed in such terms, announcing God's generous grace to the lowly and desperate.

In the Beatitudes, Jesus speaks of the "poor in spirit" and those who "hunger and thirst for righteousness" as being blessed. But in a similar passage in Luke 6:20-26, he speaks of those who are simply poor and hungry, without additional qualification. Moreover, he makes it clear that the kingdom turns typical ideas of happiness and blessing on their heads. The poor, the hungry, the distraught, the social outcasts: these are the ones, oddly, whom Jesus pronounces happy. The rich and well-fed, those who have social standing and plenty to smile about, may seem to have it made, but they have nothing to look forward to in the age to come.

Similarly, consider the story of the Annunciation, the angel Gabriel's announcement to Mary that she would be the mother of the long-awaited Messiah. Mary hurries to the home of her cousin Elizabeth, also miraculously pregnant with the child who will grow up to become John the Baptist. When Elizabeth hears Mary's voice, the baby inside her leaps for joy, and she blurts out, "God has blessed you above all women, and he has blessed the child you carry. ...Happy is she who believed that the Lord would fulfill the promises he made to her" (Luke 1:42,44). Listen to Mary's response:

> With all my heart I glorify the Lord! In the depths of who I am I rejoice in God my savior. He has looked with favor on the low status of his servant. Look! From now on, everyone will consider me highly favored because the mighty one has

> done great things for me. Holy is his name. He shows mercy to everyone, from one generation to the next, who honors him as God. He has shown strength with his arm. He has scattered those with arrogant thoughts and proud inclinations. He has pulled the powerful down from their thrones and lifted up the lowly. He has filled the hungry with good things and sent the rich away empty-handed. He has come to the aid of his servant Israel, remembering his mercy, just as he promised to our ancestors, to Abraham and to Abraham's descendants forever. –Luke 1:46-55

Her song echoes the praise of the psalmist:

> Let them thank the LORD for his faithful love and his wondrous works for all people, because God satisfied the one who was parched with thirst, and he filled up the hungry with good things! –Psalm 107:8-9

The God of Promise, a holy, mighty, and merciful God, opposes the arrogant and powerful but shows favor to the lowly. This God, Mary declares, has filled the hungry with good things and sent away the rich. To those who hunger, this is good news of a great God.

But people, unfortunately, are fickle and forgetful. Even those who gladly receive God's gifts, who praise him for his grace, may begin to lose their grip on gratitude in the face of needs that seem to go unfulfilled.

The exodus—the defining story of God's people—is a case in point. When God sent Moses to rescue Israel from slavery in Egypt, the people were oppressed and miserable, crying out desperately to God. Through Moses, the Lord did one mighty work after another, culminating in the mightiest of them all: a nighttime escape on dry ground through a miraculously divided sea (Exodus 14). In the morning, the water returned to its proper place, drowning Pharaoh's army. The Israelites looked back, saw piles of dead bodies on the seashore, and believed.

But just a handful of verses later in the story, the griping began. The people were no doubt hot and tired as they trekked through the desert, with no place to pop in for a quick Frappuccino; they began to complain to Moses of having nothing to drink (Exodus 15:22-25). And shortly after that, they complained about the lack of food, in a rather jaw-dropping fashion: "Oh, how we wish that the LORD had just put us to death while we were still in the land of Egypt. There we could sit by the pots cooking meat and eat our fill of bread" (16:3).

You would think that a people who had seen their God wipe out an entire army—and to them, an impressively powerful and high-tech army at that—would know better than to say, "Gee, if only God had put us to death." But hunger pangs can do that: we find it hard to think of anything else. We forget to say thank you for the blessings we've already received, we irritably start pointing fingers of blame, and even an oppressive past gets rewritten as a glorious feast by comparison to the needs of the present.

Despite the people's lack of gratitude, however, God responded with patience and grace. He heard their complaint and sent them quail and manna to eat (Exodus 16:11-14).

Perhaps that would take care of the grumbling?

Hardly. Apparently, quail didn't stay on the menu, only manna. And eventually, the people tired of it, again daydreaming of the good old days they left behind in Egypt. Troublemakers stir up the people. Before, the complaint had been, "We're starving—there's nothing to eat! If only we could be back in Egypt where it was all-you-can-eat every day!" They're not starving anymore, but the new complaint is, "Manna, manna, manna—we're sick and tired of manna!" They wanted meat. In their imaginations, they longed for the rich and varied Egyptian smorgasbord they left behind: fish, cucumbers, and melons, not to mention leeks, onions, and garlic. And everything, they remembered wistfully, was "free"; they forgot how they had paid for that food with backbreaking slave labor (Numbers 11:4-6).

Now before we judge the Israelites too quickly or harshly, consider: haven't we opened the door on a refrigerator or a pantry or a kitchen cabinet filled with a variety of tasty and nutritious food and complained that there was "nothing to eat"? The Israelites ate manna for 40 *years* (Exodus 16:35). How many ways could there have been to prepare it? They made cakes of it, but what else?

Manna-cotti, perhaps?

This time, however, God's anger burned against the people, because he knew their complaint to be a rejection. He had miraculously rescued them from their captivity in Egypt, and because of their unfulfilled desires, all they could think about was going back. His response, basically, was, "You want meat? I'll give you meat. I'll give you so much meat it'll come out of your noses and make you nauseous" (Numbers 11:18-20).

Be careful what you ask for. And how you ask.

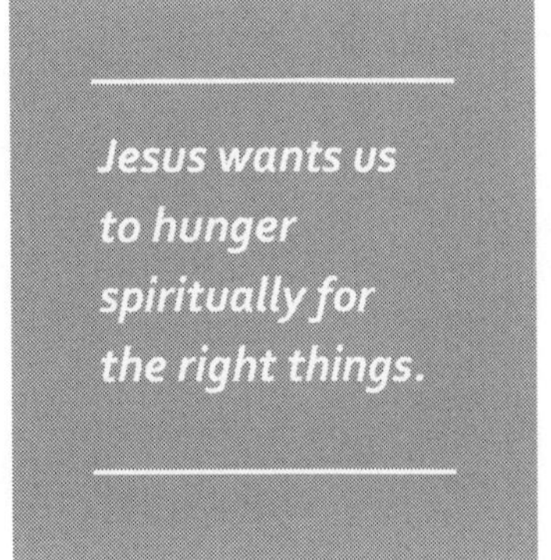
Jesus wants us to hunger spiritually for the right things.

Hunger and thirst are legitimate needs, and we have a gracious Father who knows that we need them. But Jesus wants us to stop worrying, trust God, and seek the kingdom instead (Matthew 6:31-34). It's not a matter of eliminating physical hunger altogether, but learning to hunger spiritually for the right things.

❧☙

Of course, hunger is an issue in the New Testament too. Centuries after the Israelites' conflict with God over manna, we find Jesus sitting on a hillside near the Sea of Galilee, about to perform the only one of his miracles that's recorded in all four gospels.[10]

A crowd of over 5,000 men, women, and children has come to hear him and to be healed of their sicknesses. It's getting late in the day; the disciples tell Jesus to send the people away to find food and lodging.

Jesus says no, however, and tells *them* to feed the crowd.

With what? they probably think to themselves; they object that all they have to work with is a boy's sack lunch of two small fish and five tiny barley loaves.

But Jesus receives the meager offering and blesses it. He begins to break off pieces of bread and fish and hand them to the disciples, continuing until the entire crowd has eaten its fill. Afterward, there's more food left over than the amount with which they started.

Impressed by the miracle, the people rise up to force Jesus to be their king, but he eludes them. He and the disciples cross the lake by boat, but the crowd goes the long way around and follows on foot.

Jesus knows why they have come: quite simply, they want more bread. They're not hungry for the kingdom that Jesus brings; what they want is a Messiah of the Endless Free Lunch. He tries to redirect them, but to no avail. He tells them that they must believe in him. But in response, they demand a specific and self-serving sign:

> They asked, "What miraculous sign will you do, that we can see and believe you? What will you do? Our ancestors ate manna in the wilderness, just as it is written, *He gave them bread from heaven to eat.*" –John 6:30-31

The people appear to be rather loosely quoting Psalm 78:23-24—"God...opened heaven's doors, and rained manna on them so they could eat. He gave them the very grain of heaven!" The deep irony is that the words are being taken badly out of context. The psalm is not only about the gracious provision of God, but Israel's self-centered lack of faith in response to that grace: "God gave them exactly what they craved. But they didn't stop craving—even with the food still in their mouths!" (vss. 29-30).

Jesus tries again. He tells them: "I am the bread of life. Whoever comes to me will never go hungry, and whoever believes in me will never be thirsty" (John 6:35). But they still don't understand. Instead, they begin to grumble amongst themselves: *What a terribly inappropriate thing to say—just who does this guy think he is?*

Who, indeed.

The people want literal, physical bread to feed their hungry mouths. Jesus gives himself to feed their hungry souls.

But they don't want what's on the menu.

As suggested in chapter 1, the Beatitudes are meant to be good news to the poor, hungry, and destitute, because they announce the arrival of the kingdom of a gracious manna-giving, bread-giving God. Unfortunately, the moral of these combined Old Testament and New Testament stories seems to be that when God gives us bread, we sometimes end up craving the gift more than we do the Giver.

That cannot be the way of peacemakers.

We all have wants and desires, many of them perfectly natural or justifiable. But do we want what's on God's menu?

Couples like Gene and Janna seek counseling because they want some change in their marriage relationship—which often means wanting the therapist to declare that it's the *other* spouse who need to change. Each may have a story to tell in which he or she is the unwilling victim of the other person's faults. Whether they actually say it or not, what they want is some form of justice or fairness, some change that will right what's wrong and restore balance.

Again, there is absolutely nothing wrong with wanting our marriages to be put right. And this is consistent with the kind of hunger that's appropriate to being a peacemaker. But given what we've discussed so far about the way even legitimate desire can distort our relationships to each other and to God, we should be wise and humble about how we go to a holy God to ask for justice.

Committing to What God Wants

In the Beatitudes, Jesus teaches, "Happy are people who are hungry and thirsty for righteousness, because they will be fed until they are full" (Matthew 5:6). By now, the promise in the second half of that Beatitude should be familiar: it's a refrain we've already heard from Mary and the Psalms.

But what does Jesus mean by hungering and thirsting for *righteousness*? Acing the religion exam? Winning awards for piety?

Becoming the person that others avoid because they don't feel they can be themselves around you?

Doesn't sound like much fun.

In the Bible, the word translated "righteousness" often has the sense of "right-ness" or justice. Jesus' statement, standing at the very core of the Beatitudes, is a promise that those who long to see God's justice done will one day get their wish, for that is exactly what the final fulfillment of the kingdom will bring. Everything that sin has made wrong, God will put right.

This is the hope-filled vision that draws peacemakers forward into the future, sustaining them when circumstances get difficult in the present. It's different than the way we often take righteousness—as rule-following or impression management. Even when Jesus declares that he has come to fulfill every last requirement of the Law, he still insists that the showy spirituality and hidebound legalism of the Pharisees isn't the way of God's kingdom (Matthew 5:17-20; 6:1-4).

Imagine the following scenario. It's Sunday morning, and you're late for church—again. You *hate* being late, and are getting increasingly frustrated. Without meaning to, you get a bit short-tempered with your spouse. Things get chippy in the car. Then you pull into the parking lot, get out of the car—and both of you promptly put on your best church faces.

It's easy to identify some of the wants or needs that drive this little one-act marital drama. *If only we could be on time, just once—is that really too much to ask?* Digging deeper: we want our spouse to share our concern for punctuality, to be more helpful and stop dawdling. We want a good parking space. And we want others to think well of us. Heaven forbid that anyone think we were having a fight in the car!

We want this. We want that. And there's nothing wrong with wanting to be punctual.

But where in any of this is there a hunger for true righteousness, a longing for justice? Where is the spirit that recites the Lord's Prayer and humbly says, "Father, may your will be done on earth as it is in heaven—and let it begin with me"?

At the end of chapter 2, I asked you to think about what it would take for God to look at your marriage and say, "Now that's *good.*" What would we do differently if we understood ourselves to be conduits of God's shalom at home?

Think again of the we're-late-for-church scenario above. Part of the good that God wants for our marriage is the humility required to recognize that there are two points of view. I'm annoyed because I think my spouse is dilly-dallying, but in fact my spouse is doing something that's just as important to him or her as my need for punctuality is to me. Perhaps I need to step back and try to understand what that something is, the better to show empathy and compassion.

Peacemakers want to see God's justice done, which includes doing what's right in their marriages.

Or...maybe I don't understand it and never will. Still, I may need to learn how to be more lovingly patient. And ultimately, with confidence in *God's* love and patience, maybe we can both finally drop the pious playacting and be the spiritual works in progress that we really are.

Whatever else we may want in our marriages, a peacemaker's fondest desire is to see God's justice done. That entails doing what's right in our marriages, even if it means letting go of or reprioritizing competing desires.

A similar lesson can be drawn from the Beatitude, "Happy are people who have pure hearts, because they will see God" (Matthew 5:8). The language is reminiscent of Old Testament images of being cleansed from sin. Psalm 51, for example, is attributed to King David, wracked with guilt for taking the beautiful Bathsheba as his mistress and murdering her husband to cover his tracks (2 Samuel 11). It is a prayer of deep repentance and a desire to be reconciled with God:

> Have mercy on me, God, according to your faithful love! Wipe away my wrongdoings according to your great compassion! Wash me completely clean of my guilt; purify me from my sin! ...Purify me with hyssop and I will be clean; wash me and I will be whiter than snow. Let me hear joy and celebration again; let the bones you crushed rejoice once more. Hide your face from my sins; wipe away all my guilty deeds! Create a clean heart for me, God; put a new, faithful spirit deep inside me! –Psalm 51:1-2,7-10

The psalmist is so consumed with remorse that he is suffering physically. He's prepared to go through the necessary cleansing rituals for his body, but also longs to be cleansed on the inside as well, to be given a whole new heart with which to worship God.

This earnest desire for restored integrity is the direct opposite of the religious hypocrisy for which Jesus condemned the Pharisees. They were like cups or even tombs that had been made to look beautiful on the outside, but full of all manner of detestable things on the inside, including "violence and pleasure seeking...pretense and rebellion" (Matthew 23:25-28).

Purity of heart, by contrast, is akin to whole-heartedness: it refers to a heart that is not only clean, but undivided. It's the opposite of being double-minded (James 4:8), a state in which our will and our relationships are torn by competing desires. As the 19th century philosopher Søren Kierkegaard once wrote, "Purity of heart is to will one thing."[11]

And what a peacemaker wills is what God wills: for all that is broken to be made whole, for all that is wrong to be made right.

We don't have to look far to find brokenness in relationships. Sadly, abuse and infidelity are found even in Christian marriages, and believers are quite capable of using Scripture to emotionally browbeat one another instead of answering the call to justice, humility, and compassion themselves. Sadder still, such couples—isolated by a shroud of secrecy, neglect, or ignorance—may have no community of loving friends to speak hope into their lives.

But these are not the only marriages in which hope and peace are needed. There are much more ordinary forms of injustice, mini-betrayals of our spouses that are so common as to not be recognized as the violations they really are. Here is but a partial list:

- Criticizing or saying uncomplimentary things about your spouse to others;
- Adding insult to injury by saying such things, claiming it was just a joke, then accusing your spouse of having no sense of humor;
- Realizing that you've hurt his/her feelings, but being more concerned to defend yourself against blame than to apologize or help heal the hurt;
- Refusing to listen, sometimes even treating your spouse dismissively as if you already knew everything he/she could possibly say;
- Putting your own wants and needs ahead of your spouse's without a moment's thought;
- Insisting on your "rights" without considering what's right for the relationship.

Recognize anything on the list? Do you have examples of your own that you could add? Or do you feel like saying, "Yes, but...," and then justifying yourself?

Right. Me too.

Needless to say, even if we realize we're doing such things, these can be hard habits to break. We will need, again and again, to purify our hearts and discipline our desires to want what God wants. We will need to humbly bring ourselves back before the throne of grace to have our minds renewed, replacing worldly and self-centered ways of thinking with a rich appreciation of and desire for God's good and perfect will (cf. Romans 12:1-2).

All of this requires, in Eugene Peterson's way of describing Christian discipleship, "a long obedience in the same direction."[12] And that means a robust commitment to God and to the marriage.

℘☙

Whenever I officiate a wedding, I try to speak in realistic terms of the solemn commitment the couple is making, in the sight of God and the presence of family and friends, to love and honor one another for life. There will be days when the pledge of unconditional love will be devilishly difficult to keep. Some of the people in the congregation have come up to me afterward and told me how they began thinking more deeply about their own marriages as they listened.

But in truth, I don't know how much the bride and groom actually hear. They look beautiful and serene on the outside, but inside they're often swirling with emotion, hoping nothing goes wrong, straining toward the moment when I finally pronounce them husband and wife. That's to be expected.

I do wonder, though, what path each couple will walk after the wedding. Who will keep to the promise they've made? Who won't? And why?

Here again is part of the traditional wedding vow as found in the Book of Common Prayer:

> (Name), wilt thou have this woman to thy wedded wife, to live together after God's ordinance in the holy estate of matrimony? Wilt thou love her, comfort her, honour, and keep her in sickness and in health; and forsaking all others, keep thee only unto her, so long as ye both shall live? … I, (name), take thee, (name), to my wedded wife, to have and to hold from this day forward, for better for worse, for richer for poorer, in sickness and in health, to love and to cherish, till death us do part, according to God's holy ordinance…[13]

The wording may sound outdated and archaic to our modern ears. But more than that, the vow may sound unrealistic: *What century are you living in? Do you really expect anyone to be able to say such things and mean them?*

But there's two ways for the vow to be unrealistic. One is to say the words without really believing that anything bad will happen, as if the romantic flush of the moment will easily conquer any challenge that arises. In that regard, the vow is deeply realistic: it doesn't sugar-coat the future. *You are making a choice,* the vow says, *to love this one person, for life. In so doing, you are setting aside as possibilities the others you might have chosen. You are promising to stick to this choice even through the difficulties that are sure to come: illness, financial struggles. And you do this because you believe that this is the kind of love that a holy God desires, the kind of love that a covenant God has already demonstrated to us.*

The other meaning of "unrealistic" is actually a pessimistic judgment about what's possible in a broken and sinful world such as ours. *The vow is all very nice,* the attitude goes, *for the lucky ones. But don't shackle people with lousy marriages that should never have happened in the first place.*

I would guess that most of us can probably think of marriages that we would put in that category—perhaps even our own. I've already said that I don't believe the Bible teaches that God is holding a perfect soul mate in readiness for each of his children. I'll go further: there are a number of reasons why people choose to marry, and some of those reasons are downright foolish.

Well, surely then, one might insist, *you're not going to hold people accountable for hasty decisions made in their youth!*

Yes, I am—but not for the legalistic reasons you might think. This isn't a simple matter of saying, "Tough luck! You made your bed, now sleep in it." Forsaking the possibility of divorce does not in itself guarantee peace in a marriage.

But it might make it more likely.

Scott Stanley, a Christian and a psychologist, has written extensively about two kinds of marital commitment.[14] The first is *constraint,* which on the one hand entails a sense of duty or obligation, and on the other, a sense of the costs of breaking up. Constraint commitment says, "Even if I no longer want to be married to you, the emotional, moral, social, and financial costs of divorce are too high." *Dedication* commitment, however, has to do with a more personal, internal type of motivation that is "based in thoughtful decisions to follow a certain path and give it your best."[15]

It's not either/or, but both/and. The longer we build a married life together, the more constraints we accumulate, including a shared obligation to our children. But it's personal dedication to each other and to our shared future that provides the kind of security we need to act in the best interests of the marriage itself.[16]

The spiritual problem posed by divorce isn't mere rule-breaking. The deeper and more subtle issue—confirmed by the research on commitment—is that the more we see divorce as a solution to marital problems, the harder it is to maintain the commitment needed to work on the problems in the first place.[17]

I wouldn't want constraint commitment to be the only thing keeping two Christians in a troubled marriage; that's not how I would want Jesus' words about hungering for righteousness to be construed. But if constraint can somehow empower dedication, if the commitment to stay provides a platform upon which to build peace, then so be it.

☙❧

Peacemakers need more than rules; they need a vision of peace, an understanding of righteousness that shapes and critiques our desires and confers hope for the future. The apostle Paul, I believe, supplies just the vision needed. Writing about the crucified Jesus to the church in Corinth, Paul says this:

> He died for the sake of all so that those who are alive should live not for themselves but for the one who died for them and was raised. So then, from this point on we won't recognize people by human standards. ...[I]f anyone is in Christ, that person is part of the new creation. The old things have gone away, and look, new things have arrived! All of these new things are from God, who reconciled us to himself through Christ and who gave us the ministry of reconciliation. ...We

> beg you as Christ's representatives, "Be reconciled to God!" God caused the one who didn't know sin to be sin for our sake so that through him we could become the righteousness of God. –2 Corinthians 5:15-18,20-21

Jesus died for you to be the righteousness of God, to embody justice here and now.

Here again we have the hope-filled vision of new creation. God's kingdom, manifested in the cross and resurrection, turns the old ways of thinking about people upside-down. "If anyone is in Christ," Paul says. The implication is, *and that means you! You are in Christ, you are part of the new thing that God is doing, part of the ministry of reconciliation of which I, Paul, am an ambassador. It begins with what God has done to restore a right relationship between us and him; it plays out through your right relationships with each other.*

Right relationships: that's the embodiment of righteousness. Don't miss what Paul says. Jesus died, not just so you could get to heaven when you die, but so you could be an agent of heaven here on earth. Jesus died, not just for you to long for God's justice to descend by itself, but for you to *be* the righteousness of God, to embody justice here, now, today.

In your church. In your community.

In your marriage.

Again, there are many things we want in life. There may also be many things we want for our marriages, including the ones we promised each other when we made our wedding vows. Some of our desires are right and good: spouses *should* want to be loved and cherished, to be treated with honor and respect, to be understood.

But there are two questions we must always ask: "Do I really want what God wants?" and "Am I *doing* what God wants, or am I just waiting for my spouse to get it right first?"

The Bible teaches that "Those who make peace sow the seeds of justice (or righteousness) by their peaceful acts" (James 3:18). Is that our vision? Is that our enduring desire, the overarching goal that lends purpose and meaning even to the changes we might pray for and make in relationship to our spouses?

Happy are people who are hungry and thirsty for righteousness, who are committed to seeking God's kingdom and righteousness even at home. And as we'll see in the next two chapters, that commitment will require us to follow Jesus on the path of humility. Just remember: amidst all the desires we have in life, including the changes we'd like to see in our marriages, if we don't really want what God wants, if we don't desire God's peace and all it may require of us, the call to humility probably won't make much sense.

℘☙

Questions for discussion and reflection:

1. Read James 4:1-3 aloud. What desires battle inside you and contribute to conflicts in your marriage?

2. Consider the story of Gene and Janna's conflict over money, in which the expectations they had before marriage didn't match their married reality. Have you had expectations about married life that were disappointed? Try to state the expectation as clearly as possible, as well as what happened to disappoint you. Does your spouse know or understand?

3. God gave his people manna in the wilderness, and has given the bread of life in Jesus himself. But put yourself in the shoes of the wandering Israelites, or the people Jesus fed miraculously. What grace have you taken for granted? What unfulfilled hunger, particularly in your marriage, makes it more difficult to be grateful for God's gifts, and how?

4. Give personal examples, if possible, of the "mini-betrayals" described earlier. Don't just focus on your spouse's behavior; ask God to remind you of things *you* have done. What makes these behaviors "betrayals"? What would be a more just or righteous alternative to each?

5. Here again is the passage from 2 Corinthians 5, but rewritten in the first person. Read it out loud, slowly, and with as much conviction as you can:

> He died for my sake so that I, who am alive, should live not for myself but for the one who died for me and was raised. So then, from this point on I won't recognize people by human standards. ...[I]f anyone is in Christ, that person is part of the new creation. The old things have gone away, and look, new things have arrived! God caused the one who didn't know sin to be sin for my sake so that through him I could become the righteousness of God.

What are the implications of the biblical theme of "new creation" and of personally *being* the righteousness of God for your marriage? What hope, if any, do you find in these ideas?

5

GRACE TO THE HUMBLE

Up to this point, we've been looking at peacemaking from a big picture perspective, immersing our imaginations in the hope-filled story of God's ongoing work of renewal. Peacemaking at home requires that we commit ourselves to wanting what God wants, even in our marriages. In this chapter and the next, we'll dig more deeply into the virtue perspective with which we began, to get at the fundamental role of humility in marriage.

ஐ

Both my wife and my mother immigrated to the United States from countries wracked by war. In such war-torn environments, humility is a rare virtue, one that many might consider irrelevant. But whether in the war between nations or the fights between spouses, humility is the first step toward peace. Proverbs 15:1 states wisely that "A sensitive answer turns back wrath, but an offensive word stirs up anger." In the midst of conflict, who will be the one to step back, stay calm, and give that gentle answer? Who will humbly defer the burning desire to strike back, to put others in their place, to verbally accuse and attack?

John Paul Lederach tells the following story. The West African nation of Ghana had a long history of tribal conflict, sometimes exacerbated by Christian missionary activity that changed the balance of power. In 1995, violence broke out between the largely Muslim

Dagombas, and the Konkombas, who had converted to Christianity. The fight, as usual, was over land and resources, and quickly became lethal as it radiated outward from the small town where the conflict began. The whole of northern Ghana was threatened with civil war, and a team of African mediators was sent to intervene.

The Dagombas carried a proud tradition of royal rule through a system of tribal chieftains. The Konkombas, however, were a more scattered group comprised mostly of farmers, and therefore stereotyped by the chiefly tribes as far less worthy of respect.

The mediation process began poorly and seemed doomed to fail. The Dagomban high chief, in full ceremonial garb and surrounded by an entourage of servants, immediately humiliated his rival by using words suggesting that it was below his dignity to even be in the same room to negotiate with someone of so little status.

The mediators felt trapped. They dared not disrespect the chief by criticizing him or reminding him to obey the ground rules of negotiation. And they were understandably apprehensive when the Konkomban asked permission to respond.

But surprisingly, this is what the young man said:

> You are perfectly right, Father; we do not have a chief. We have not had one for years. …And this has been our problem. The reason we react, the reason our people go on rampages and fights resulting in all these killings and destruction arises from this fact. We do not have what you have. It is really not about the town, or the land… I beg you, listen to my words, Father. I am calling you Father because we do not wish to disrespect you. You are a great chief. But what is left to us? Do we have no other means but this violence to receive in return the one thing we seek, to be respected and to establish our own chief who could indeed speak with you, rather than having a young boy do it on our behalf?[1]

The Dagomban chieftain fell silent; the haughty demeanor dissolved. Previously, the chief had addressed his remarks more to the mediators than to his rival. But now, with the arrogance gone from his voice, he addressed the young Konkomban honestly and directly:

> I had come to put your people in your place. But now I feel only shame. Though I insulted your people, you still called me Father. It is you who spoke with wisdom, and me who has not seen the truth. What you have said is true. We who are chiefly have always looked down on you because you have no chief, but we have not understood the denigration you suffered. I beg you, my son, to forgive me.[2]

Never, never underestimate the peacemaking power of humble and sensitive words.

> ***Never underestimate the peacemaking power of humble and sensitive words.***

Though the Dagomban chief had blatantly and intentionally insulted the honor of his would-be adversary, the Konkomban refused to respond in kind. Quite the contrary, he embodied a humble way of relating by avoiding defensiveness, giving the chief proper respect, and even admitting his own violence and lowliness.

He did not, however, refrain from seeking justice or speaking the truth. He simply used gentle words that were neither vengeful nor harsh. Imagine what might have happened instead if he had cried out in anger, "You don't respect us!" The chief would likely have sneered that the Konkombas were unworthy of respect, and the meeting would have been over. But when the truth was delivered in such a humble frame, the chief was able to hear it and repent.

None of this is meant to reduce humility to a mere negotiating tactic. But the story does suggest that humility may be the most basic building block in the process of making peace.

☙❧

Now imagine a simpler and more typical conflict: not full-scale tribal warfare, but the small scale skirmishes that happen in our homes. Remember Danny and Celia from chapter 1? Among other things, Celia was constantly annoyed that Danny could never remember to pick up his dirty socks and put them in the laundry.

Their neighbors, Tracey and Ted, have struggled for years with a similar small but bothersome issue. Tracey likes a clean kitchen: shiny surfaces, a place for everything, and everything in its place. Ted fancies himself a cook, but never works from a recipe: cooking is a creative, make-it-up-as-you-go process that tends to leave the kitchen in glorious chaos.

Both spouses work full-time, despite growing up in families with working fathers, and stay-at-home moms who did the cooking and cleaning. From Ted's perspective, his culinary contribution is a win-win: he gets to indulge his creativity in a way that also helps with the household chores. What he can't understand is why Tracey doesn't seem more appreciative. He tries to clean up after himself, but she never seems satisfied with what he's done.

For her part, Tracey does appreciate Ted's willingness to cook—but feels unappreciated herself for everything *she* does around the house, which in her estimation is far greater than his contribution. And she can't understand why Ted doesn't see what she sees. Doesn't he notice that the saltshaker is still sitting out? That he's left the crumpled dishrag on the counter? That the counter itself, though quickly and partially cleaned, still looks smeary and greasy in spots?

Both want appreciation, and at some level, both are willing to give it. But their history of feeling *un*-appreciated makes them overly sensitive to new slights, and it doesn't take much to trigger their defensiveness.

Ted's preparing a special meal, and Tracey walks into the kitchen. She doesn't say anything about the mess, but merely looks quickly about her and softly sighs. Ted is immediately offended. When Tracey asks what she thinks is an innocent question, he snaps back a curt reply. Now it's her turn to be offended. *What did I do to deserve that?* she wonders with resentment, silently congratulating herself for having had the self-control to not comment on the mess.

Who's right?

That's a natural question to ask, but in this case, not a very helpful one. Both of them feel justified in their anger. Both are thinking in black and white terms: I'm right, you're wrong. And both are contributing to the kind of endless back-and-forth conflict in which so many couples feel trapped. *I want you to respect me, to appreciate me, to understand me. But I'm the victim here, so I'll only respect you when I'm sure that you respect me.* When both spouses think that way, nothing changes, because neither is willing to make the first move of giving the other the loving respect they're due.

A more humble attitude on either side would help. Tracey can express appreciation for Ted's creative contributions in the kitchen, and even his attempts at cleanup—without having to abandon her standards of cleanliness. And Ted doesn't have to understand Tracey's need for an immaculate kitchen; he only needs to accept that this is important to her, while simultaneously noticing and thanking her for all the things she does to keep their home running smoothly.

In the next chapter, we'll explore further some practical expressions of humility that can help break through the negative cycles of interaction that trouble so many marriages. If warring tribes can do it, so can we! But first, let's return again to the Beatitudes for some perspective.

The Humiliation of Weakness

When you think of a humble person, what image comes to mind? As Brett Scharffs has written, "Of all virtues, none needs a public relations consultant more than humility," because it is generally perceived as the "loser's virtue of wimps and doormats."[3] We may have unappealing images of people who don't know how to stand up for themselves, who are continually victimized by manipulative or selfish people. Nor is this solely a modern prejudice: even Aristotle, to whom we owe much in the philosophy of virtue, disdained humility as "a sad reality of biological and social inferiority."[4]

Ask yourself honestly: is there some part of you that feels the same way? Does the thought of learning to be more humble carry with it the implied threat of having others take advantage of you? Perhaps there are people whose humility you admire; perhaps you were moved as I was by the story of the Konkomban delegate. But when it comes right down to it, you may not really want more humility in your life.

And when you think of your relationship with your spouse, humility may be the last thing for which you pray.

It's a tough sell. As we've seen, in the Beatitudes, Jesus says that those who are hopeless, grieving, humble, and hungering for justice are happy, while in Luke 6:20-21, it's those who are poor, hungry, and weeping who are blessed. That sounds more like humiliation than happiness, weakness and powerlessness instead of the kind of strength and self-reliance that has been honored by so many cultures through the ages. Furthermore, some have taken Jesus' words as commanding Christians to be doormats in any and every situation, as when a wife is told by her husband or even her pastor that it is her spiritual duty to obey whatever her husband says, even in situations of physical or emotional abuse.

But that's not what Jesus meant.

Again, why are the Beatitudes good news? It's not because being hopeless or poor, humble or hungry, brings a wealth of positive emotions. And it's not because God wants people to be poor and hungry. Rather, the news is good because it announces the arrival of the kingdom of a good God, one who champions those who are powerless, oppressed, and downtrodden.

Long ago, the prophet Isaiah wrote:

> From ancient times, no one has heard, no ear has perceived,
> no eye has seen any god but you who acts on behalf of those
> who wait for him! –Isaiah 64:4

Jesus' proclamation of the kingdom declares that the wait is over. That's the good news: but it's important that we welcome the kingdom he actually brought. If God is on the side of those who have been humbled in life, then we need to line our attitudes up with his purposes. We may not be powerless, but we need to use what power we have in appropriately humble ways. Throughout Scripture, we find this theme: "God stands against the proud, but he gives favor to the humble" (James 4:6; 1 Peter 5:5). Those who are wise know the dangers of pride:

> Pride comes before disaster, and arrogance before a fall. Better to be humble with the needy than to divide plunder with the proud. –Proverbs 16:18-19

Story after biblical story illustrates the truth that pride goes before a fall. When kings and leaders, whether inside or outside the people of God, become drunk with power and pride, disaster ensues.

Pharaoh, ruler of ancient Egypt, is a prime example. Confronted by the miraculous might of God through the miracles performed by Moses, he finally obeys God's demand to "Let my people go." But once they've gone, he has second thoughts and gives chase, unwilling to accept his humiliation. Tragically, his pride costs the lives of the entire Egyptian army.

It's easy to mock Pharaoh's foolish arrogance. But there is a danger in doing so, one that dogs any meaningful discussion of humility and pride. In fact, one of my hesitations in using the language of virtue in this book at all is because it's too easily co-opted by religious pride: *Learn these virtues and become a real Christian! Be one of the few that gets it right!* It's for similar reasons that Paul had to correct the attitude of believers in the city of Corinth who had become proud of their spiritual gifts and their supposed wisdom:

> Look at your situation when you were called, brothers and sisters! By ordinary human standards not many were wise, not many were powerful, not many were from the upper

> class. But God chose what the world considers foolish to shame the wise. God chose what the world considers weak to shame the strong. And God chose what the world considers low-class and low-life—what is considered to be nothing—to reduce what is considered to be something to nothing. So no human being can brag in God's presence. ...Who says that you are better than anyone else? What do you have that you didn't receive? And if you received it, then why are you bragging as if you didn't receive it?
>
> –1 Corinthians 1:26-29; 4:7

It might also help to remember the parable Jesus told to those who were convinced of their moral superiority:

> Two people went up to the temple to pray. One was a Pharisee and the other a tax collector. The Pharisee stood and prayed about himself with these words, "God, I thank you that I'm not like everyone else—crooks, evildoers, adulterers—or even like this tax collector. I fast twice a week. I give a tenth of everything I receive." But the tax collector stood at a distance. He wouldn't even lift his eyes to look toward heaven. Rather, he struck his chest and said, "God, show mercy to me, a sinner." I tell you, this person went down to his home justified rather than the Pharisee. All who lift themselves up will be brought low, and those who make themselves low will be lifted up. –Luke 18:10-14

We may be used to thinking of the Pharisees as villains in the gospel stories. In all likelihood, however, many of the people who heard Jesus' parables would have considered the Pharisees as religious models, while tax gatherers were traitors, the lowest of the low. Thus, for Jesus' audience at least, the moral of the story shockingly reversed expectations: it's the proud Pharisee who will be humbled, and the lowly tax-gatherer who will be lifted up by God for his humility.

Jesus told a similar parable when he was at a dinner party and noticed the guests jockeying for position, trying to get the places of honor at the table:

> When someone invites you to a wedding celebration, don't take your seat in the place of honor. Someone more highly regarded than you could have been invited by your host. The host who invited both of you will come and say to you, "Give your seat to this other person." Embarrassed, you will take your seat in the least important place. Instead, when you receive an invitation, go and sit in the least important place. When your host approaches you, he will say, "Friend, move up here to a better seat." Then you will be honored in the presence of all your fellow guests. All who lift themselves up will be brought low, and those who make themselves low will be lifted up. –Luke 14:8-11

It would be a terrible distortion to read Jesus as recommending a better strategy to avoid embarrassment and get the honor one craves. He was speaking into a society in which such things are taken for granted and matter deeply, and pointing them toward another reality, a kingdom in which all such values are turned upside down. For us, the lesson is: *Don't humble yourself as a way to get noticed; as peacemakers, do it because it's the way of God's kingdom, and because what truly matters is to be honored by <u>him</u>.*

Is pride really such a bad thing? There can be an appropriate place for pride, as R. T. Kendall suggests: "We need to take ourselves seriously to some extent." But the danger is in "taking oneself *too* seriously," and the line between them is fine indeed.[5]

Appropriate pride will allow us to take pleasure in any use of personal power that promotes justice and flourishing.[6] Let's say, for example, that I make a conscious choice to set aside my anger or frustration long enough to actually listen attentively to my wife. If that choice actually leads to deeper understanding or connection, I have every reason to celebrate that fact and to want to do even better.

But if I start keeping score, if I start thinking "Why do I have to listen to her when she doesn't listen to me?" and resenting it, I've crossed the line. This is pride gone wrong: no longer is it about rejoicing in what's right and good, but taking refuge in my supposed superiority over someone else.

In other words, if any virtue is pursued in a spirit of improper pride instead of with humility and a hunger for righteousness, it will eventually be for naught. As the 19th century South African minister Andrew Murray once wrote:

> Humility, the place of entire dependence on God, is, from the very nature of things, the first duty and the highest virtue of the creature, and the root of every virtue. …It is the only soil in which the graces root…because it alone takes the right attitude before God, and allows Him as God to do all.[7]

The virtues can only be cultivated properly in the rich soil of humility. God consistently chooses the humble and lowly to accomplish his purposes. Moses, for example, was a humble man (Numbers 12:3) who couldn't fathom why God would choose him to be his representative: "Who am I to go to Pharaoh and to bring the Israelites out of Egypt?" (Exodus 3:11). God's answer was not, "Moses, I've reviewed your work history, and you're clearly the man for the job." His response, rather, was, "I'll be with you" (vs. 12).

Or consider the story of Gideon. For seven years, God allowed the disobedient Israelites to be oppressed by the Midianites. Finally, God sent an angel to commission Gideon to deliver Israel. Uncertain if the messenger really was from God, Gideon replied, "With all due respect, my Lord, how can I rescue Israel? My clan is the weakest in Manasseh, and I'm the youngest in my household" (Judges 6:15). God's response echoes the one given Moses above: "Because I'm with you, you'll defeat the Midianites as if they were just one person" (vs. 16). And God sent Gideon into battle with only 300 men against vastly superior forces, to keep the Israelites from thinking they had accomplished the impossible on their own (Judges 7:2).

Having triumphantly brought the ark of God to Jerusalem, King David deeply desired to build a temple for God to dwell in. But through the prophet Nathan, God told him no, vowing instead to establish David's dynasty; one of his own children would build the temple. Hearing the promise, David humbly responded, "Who am I, LORD God, and of what significance is my family that you have brought me this far?" (2 Samuel 7:18).

The apostle Paul was once a proud man: he was well-educated, well-born, and a zealous persecutor of early Christians. Then he was confronted by the resurrected Jesus, and everything changed. Imagine the spiritual whiplash, the blow suffered to his self-righteous certainty. To put it in contemporary terms, he crumpled up his religious résumé and flushed it down the toilet (Philippians 3:5-8), to give his life to the one he had previously persecuted.

These were not flawless men. Gideon repeatedly needed signs from God to believe what he had been told. David's sins are well known. Moses could be willful and short-tempered, and so could Paul.

As we saw in chapter 3, the Bible is full of stories in which God summons ordinary human beings with all their weaknesses and faults to stand before kings and empires. The biblical response to that call is often, "Who, me?"

For that reason, I sometimes think of humility as "who-me-lity": the disposition that answers God's summons with an earnest, "But who am I, Lord?" instead of "Well, it's about time you called."

> ***Humility is "who-me-lity": the disposition that answers God's summons with, "But who am I, Lord?"***

God may commission us to do things we don't think we can do, even things we don't *want* to do, including making peace. Anything we do to strengthen our marriages must begin with humility: a faithful submission to the will of a peacemaking God.

In the world's eyes, that submission might seem like weakness. But in the eyes of a humble God, that's strength.

Humility as Strength from God

Imagine the apostle Paul sitting in prison, writing a letter to the Gentile church in the Roman colony of Philippi. These people are his dearly beloved friends whom he considers to be "partners in the ministry of the gospel" (Philippians 1:5). Paul knows them to be a cohesive and resilient congregation, but seems concerned that they stick together in the face of recent troubles that he doesn't name (most likely, persecution).

Thus, as he writes, he tells them what would make him really happy as he sits in his cell, praying and contemplating. He lays before them a rich vision of church unity:

> Therefore, if there is any encouragement in Christ, any comfort in love, any sharing in the Spirit, any sympathy, complete my joy by thinking the same way, having the same love, being united, and agreeing with each other. Don't do anything for selfish purposes, but with humility think of others as better than yourselves. Instead of each person watching out for their own good, watch out for what is better for others.
>
> –Philippians 2:1-4

"If," he says, which probably means "since." He's describing things that are already true of them, but that they need to continue doing wholeheartedly to maintain their unity. "Thinking the same way" and "agreeing with one another" doesn't mean that they must have identical opinions on everything or vote the same way on church decisions. I like to think of it as having their moral compasses pointed in the same direction, toward a common vision.

And in that vision, humility plays a central role. Contrasting it with selfishness, Paul describes humble people not as "looking out for number one," but looking out for each other.

He tells them to think of others as better than themselves. This isn't because each person is actually everyone else's social inferior; that would be nonsensical. Nor does he say, "Think of others as better, because you're a worthless worm anyway." Valuing others doesn't mean devaluing ourselves[8]—though as we'll see in the next chapter, humility *does* require recognizing the self-serving ways we compare ourselves to others.

Rather, as he does so often, Paul backs up his moral instruction by giving the broader perspective. Why should they be humble in this way? Because they follow a humble savior who put the needs of others before himself. Quoting what may have been an early Christian hymn, Paul writes:

> Adopt the attitude that was in Christ Jesus:
> Though he was in the form of God,
> he did not consider being equal with God something to exploit.
> But he emptied himself
> by taking the form of a slave
> and by becoming like human beings.
> When he found himself in the form of a human,
> he humbled himself by becoming obedient to the point of death,
> even death on a cross.
> Therefore, God highly honored him
> and gave him a name above all names,
> so that at the name of Jesus everyone
> in heaven, on earth, and under the earth might bow
> and every tongue confess
> that Jesus Christ is Lord,
> to the glory of God the Father.
>
> –Philippians 2:5-11

These can be mind-bending words if we stop long enough to consider what they actually mean. Jesus was nobody's inferior: he was equal to God. And what do we associate with divinity? Power and majesty? Holiness and justice? I haven't tried this experiment yet, but I would guess that if I were to ask a roomful of Christians to list the so-called "attributes of God," few if any would say, "humility."

To the extent that we associate humility with intrinsic weakness, this probably won't be part of our concept of God. But as theologian William Placher has rightly insisted regarding the passage from Philippians above:

> This is what God is like, not as a mere message from God, information passed on, but as God's own self come among us as the revelation of who God is.[9]

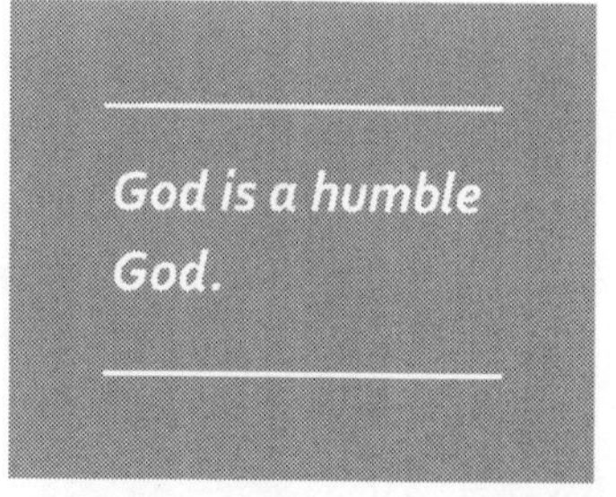

Jesus showed us what God is like, by emptying himself, not of goodness, but privilege. Jesus saves because Jesus serves; Jesus serves because God is by nature a humble God.

This should stop us short whenever we're tempted to think of humility as weakness, as some kind of deficit. To regard humility as the "loser's virtue" is to think as much of the world does in its pursuit of power, influence, and social success. But as Robert Roberts has suggested:

> the opposite of humility as a virtue is not self-confidence, initiative, assertiveness, and self-esteem, but instead pushiness, scorn of "inferiors," rejoicing in the downfall of others, envy, resentment and grudge-bearing, ruthless ambition, haughtiness, shame at failure or disadvantageous comparison, and the need to excel [over] others so as to think well of oneself.[10]

Think honestly of that list of negative qualities with respect to your marriage. Do you ever push to get your own way? Have you ever treated your spouse with scorn or contempt? Have you taken secret (or perhaps not so secret) pleasure in seeing your spouse "get what was coming" to him or her?

You get the idea.

Humility is not the opposite of self-confidence: it is *empowered* by self-confidence, by not having to prove or defend ourselves. Why do we push, whine at, and manipulate others? Because we don't trust them to hear us and cooperate. Why do we look down at our spouses with self-righteous contempt? Because we feel the need to raise ourselves above them. Why do we bear grudges and "keep a record of complaints" (1 Corinthians 13:6)? To protect ourselves from being hurt again; we wear our resentment like armor.

Humility may sound like weakness. But the biblical perspective is that true humility is divine strength. God is humble—not powerless, not weak. To the extent that we embody that humility in our lives and relationships, we reflect the character of God, just as peacemakers will be known as God's true children (Matthew 5:9).

And there's more. When it comes to learning humility, we're not left to our own devices. Having told the Philippians to humbly care for each other's needs, and immediately after having pointed them lyrically to the example of Jesus, Paul writes this:

> Therefore, my loved ones, just as you always obey me, not just when I am present but now even more while I am away, carry out your own salvation with fear and trembling. God is the one who enables you both to want and to actually live out his good purposes. –Philippians 2:12-13

"Carry out your own salvation with fear and trembling." If humility sounds to us like an impossible religious burden, then this command may seem frightening. We know that God champions the humble and stands against the proud; is Paul saying that failures of humility may cause us to lose our salvation?

Quite the contrary. Paul is writing to a group of people in whom he has great confidence, and encouraging them to continue on their journey of spiritual growth. He is not, therefore, threatening them with divine punishment for bad behavior, as if to say, "Be humble, or forfeit your salvation." He's saying, "You've been saved by the grace of a humble God; just make sure that you keep embodying the truth and reality of that salvation in your humble way of living."

But why "fear and trembling"? Because of the astonishing truth of what he says next. God doesn't just put moral demands on us from afar; he works in and through us, giving us the power both to want what he wants and to do it. It's not either/or: either we obey God on our own, or he manipulates us as if we were mere puppets. It's both/and: we are commanded to humble, *and* enabled to do so.

Think about what this means. The God of the universe, the one who hung the stars in their places (e.g., Genesis 1:14-18; Job 38:31-32; Psalm 8:3-4) continues to demonstrate his humility by living in us through his Holy Spirit (e.g., Romans 8:9-11; 1 Corinthians 3:16; Ephesians 2:22).

Have some of us become so used to that idea that we take it for granted, and cease to be amazed by it? If we truly understood what Paul was saying, would we not tremble? Not with terror, perhaps, but with the awe appropriate to recognizing the divine power that indwells a life of humility.

❧☙

There's simply not much encouragement in our world to live humbly. It may always have been this way, considering the attention Jesus gave to humility in word and deed. It's not just the Beatitudes. He taught his disciples to follow his own humble example, promising that in so doing they would find rest from their strivings (Matthew 11:28-30). He taught them to stop being ambitious in a worldly way, and to become humble like children instead (Matthew 18:1-4). And mere days before his arrest and crucifixion, he rode into Jerusalem on the back of a donkey, fulfilling an ancient prophecy that the Messiah would come as a humble man of peace instead of war (Matthew 21:5; Zechariah 9:9).

Jesus has given us both a command to live humbly and an example to follow. And we have his Spirit, who enables us to let go of our selfish tendencies (Romans 8:5-13). We therefore have no excuse.

But again, we need to welcome the kingdom that Jesus actually brought. He's not saying, "Be humble, or God'll get you." He's not saying, "If you want to get into God's kingdom, you'd better get this humility thing right first." Rather, the Beatitudes teach that the kingdom comes as a gift. God favors the humble, because God himself is humble and gracious.

No doubt, where marital trust has been eroded, where spouses have repeatedly hurt one another, humility may sound like a burdensome obligation. Don't we need to protect ourselves? Doesn't humility put us at risk of being hurt again? The fear of powerlessness and pain makes humility seem like bad advice.

In speaking of humility as a foundational virtue, it's not my intent to set up a list of moral rules that separates "good" Christians from bad, obedient from disobedient, regardless of circumstances. The point, rather, is that peacemakers need the hope-filled imagination to envision what God may want to do to bring peace to our marriages, the desire to see God's will done, and the humility to submit to his purposes.

Humility is not powerlessness, but the faithful use of power in the service of peacemaking.

Is it risky? Yes. Anything we do in a broken world, even in the pursuit of peace, involves risk. But the Bible asks us to faithfully imagine ourselves, as Paul did, as ambassadors of a king who desires to bring reconciliation to the world (2 Corinthians 5:18-20). As a virtue, true humility is not mere powerlessness, but the faithful use of power in the service of peacemaking.

And what does humility in marriage look like? We'll explore some possibilities in the next chapter.

ꕥ

Questions for discussion and reflection:

1. Reread the story of Tracey and Ted. Do you identify with either of them, and if so, how? In what way is each of them justified in feeling offended by the other's behavior? Thinking of Proverbs 15:1, what "sensitive answer" could each give in response to the offense?

2. If you know one, tell a story about a person who tried to respond humbly to a situation but suffered as a consequence. Did you admire what that person did, or think him or her foolish (or a little of both)? If that person had come to you for advice or encouragement, what would you have said? What do your answers tell you about your understanding of humility?

3. Conversely, tell a true story that illustrates the proverb that "Pride goes before destruction, and a haughty spirit before a fall" (Proverbs 16:18, New King James Version). In that story, was there any part of pride that might have been legitimate or appropriate? If so, what was it, and where did it go wrong?

4. Now apply the same ideas to your marriage relationship. What role might pride play in your marital conflicts? Don't focus on your spouse's pride, but your own. What part of that pride is appropriate? Why? And where does it go wrong?

5. Does the call to be humble in your marriage feel risky to you? In what way? What hope or encouragement, if any, do you draw from Paul's words in Philippians 2:12-13, that God is at work in you both to want and to do his will?

6

AT HOME WITH HUMILITY

The previous chapter sketched a big-picture view of humility and its role in the Christian life. As the Beatitudes suggest, the coming of God's kingdom is good news because God in his inexplicable grace blesses those who have been humbled by life. But God is also humble by nature, without being weak, and those who follow Christ are called to embody that humility in their life together. In this chapter, we'll consider what humility in marriage might look like in practical terms, beginning with the matter of pride.

꧁꧂

It doesn't take much to wound our pride (well, *mine* anyway). My wife and I recently received an advertising circular from a company that does custom paving work for homeowners. Their less-than-slick slogan, printed on the envelope in bold letters, was: "We buy ugly driveways, and we want yours!" My automatic first thought was a slightly defensive one: *That's a tad insulting, isn't it? You haven't even seen my driveway.* And the second? *It's a good thing these folks aren't selling cosmetic surgery. What an ad campaign that would be.*

If someone we don't even know can tweak our pride from a distance, imagine what someone close to us—like a spouse—can do.

Like Ted in the last chapter, I enjoy being creative in the kitchen, taking personal pride in being able to spontaneously fuse whatever ingredients we already have in our refrigerator and cabinets into a decent meal. For that reason, I find recipes constraining, and use them for inspiration rather than instruction. Sometimes, I don't even bother to taste the food as I go (celebrity chef Gordon Ramsay would be sputtering with disbelief), adding a splash of this and a sprinkle of that, trusting that everything will be just fine.

What that means, of course, is that my creations sometimes flop. Badly. (Score one for Ramsay.)

One time, my wife came into the kitchen as I was happily slinging seasonings. "Don't you think that's enough salt?" she asked evenly, trying not to show alarm.

I could have responded with equal poise: "Yes, that seems to be about right," or "No, actually, I think it probably needs a bit more." But I was immediately on the defensive; I knew this wasn't really a question. She wasn't asking for information, but voicing an opinion: "Sweetie, I think that's enough salt."

And although I hate to say it, the implied criticism injured my sense of creative competence. Part of me knew that she was probably right; I was being rather liberal with the salt, and it would have been wise to at least stop and do a taste test. But another part of me refused to admit the possibility that I had made a mistake.

If I had remained calm, I might have remembered that she actually enjoyed and appreciated my cooking in general. And I might have realized that she wasn't looking for an opportunity to criticize, but was anxious about the fact that I was cooking for company, who wouldn't enjoy the meal if I made it too salty. "Don't you think that's enough salt?" was code for "I'm worried that the meal might bomb, and that would be unpleasant for everyone."

I don't remember exactly what I said or did, but I'm fairly certain that it didn't involve humility. I made the situation all about me, ignoring what was best for her or our guests. Knowing myself, I would have thought about rebelliously shaking even *more* salt into the food just to show that I could. More likely, though, I would have put the saltshaker down with an exaggerated flourish, thrown my hands in the air, stepped back from the stove, and asked sarcastically, "Maybe *you* would like to do the cooking?"

Childish? Yes. Unhelpful? Definitely.

Humble? Not even close.

But be honest: haven't you done something similar? Even if we have a big picture perspective of humility, getting a practical handle on how to live it out in our marriages still requires recognizing and dealing with injured pride.

What's So Bad About Pride?

> *Getting a practical handle on humility in marriage requires dealing with injured pride.*

In Christian tradition, pride is not only one of the so-called "seven deadly sins," it's been considered to be the deadliest or most basic. If, as suggested by the earlier quote from Andrew Murray, humility is the root of all virtue, then the reverse may also be true: "pride, or the loss of this humility, is the root of every sin and evil."[1]

My concern, however, is that if there are one-dimensional and distorted ways of thinking about humility as wimpiness, so too are there unhelpful stereotypes of pride. Certainly, in some marriages, one or both of the spouses are overbearing, self-centered, insufferable narcissists (no names or finger pointing, please), making life understandably difficult. But this may be only an extreme version of a more usual problem: the defensive kind of pride in which our sense of value as a person depends too much and too delicately on the behavior and opinions of others, particularly our spouses. We may be able to wave off the minor insults we think those outside our home have inflicted on us. But it's harder to do this when it's the person we live with day in and day out, the one whom we depend on for better or worse.

We can begin by recognizing that pride is frequently condemned in Scripture. The book of Proverbs, for example, consistently warns against pride, holding up humility as the godly alternative (e.g., Proverbs 11:2; 18:12; 29:23). Wisdom, personified as a woman, echoes the Beatitudes when she says, "Now children, listen to me: happy are those who keep to my ways!" (Proverbs 8:32), and those ways include hating proud and arrogant speech (8:13). "Arrogance" describes those who take something that doesn't belong to them, claiming power or status that isn't rightly theirs. Thus, sinful pride is not just taking ourselves too seriously, but taking ourselves more seriously than we do God—in essence, a form of idolatry.

There are obvious forms of idolatrous arrogance, as when the enemies of God scoff recklessly at him and at his people. But pride comes in more subtle forms as well. When the prophets speak of God bringing down the proud and haughty, for example, the condemnation includes God's own people (e.g., Isaiah 9:8-12; Ezekiel 7:24), especially when they have forgotten their dependence upon his providential care (e.g., Hosea 13:6).

That's why Moses, as the people of Israel prepare to enter the promised land, warns them not to forget the God who rescued them from Egypt. He begins with a positive command:

> Love the LORD your God with all your heart, all your being, and all your strength. These words that I am commanding you today must always be on your minds. Recite them to your children. Talk about them when you are sitting around your house and when you are out and about, when you are lying down and when you are getting up. Tie them on your hand as a sign. They should be on your forehead as a symbol. Write them on your house's doorframes and on your city's gates. –Deuteronomy 6:5-9

Recite the commandments. Tell the stories. Talk about them daily as a family. Do whatever you need to do to remember what God has done, and how you have been blessed because of it. That is the ground of proper humility, the hedge against improper pride.

Why is the command necessary? Won't the people always remember the marvelous, miraculous provision of God? In a word, no. Moses seems to know that once the people get settled, once the memory of their previous hardships has faded, they will begin to take the blessing for granted and forget the God who brought them there:

> Now once the LORD your God has brought you into the land that he swore to your ancestors, to Abraham, Isaac, and Jacob, to give to you—a land that will be full of large and wonderful towns that you didn't build, houses stocked with all kinds of goods that you didn't stock, cisterns that you didn't make, vineyards and olive trees that you didn't plant—and you eat and get stuffed, watch yourself! Don't forget the LORD, who brought you out of Egypt, out of the house of slavery. –Deuteronomy 6:10-12

Moses seems to say, "You're about to enjoy a huge increase in your standard of living. You're going to be comfortable and well-fed. So don't forget who's responsible for your good fortune. Don't take credit where none is due: *you didn't do a thing to deserve it.*"

Would Moses have needed to say the same thing to us?

It's one thing to feel oppressed and hopeless, poor in spirit and humiliated by life. When that happens, we cry out to God in utter dependence. But if and when we finally find ourselves in the promised land (or a reasonable facsimile thereof), we may begin to forget, and in the forgetting become proud and arrogant, thinking that we somehow deserve everything we have.

Don't forget, Moses warns. *Remember what God has done, and love him with everything you've got.*

℘℘

Pride, therefore, isn't somebody else's problem—it's ours, yours and mine. As C. S. Lewis once wrote, in his usual succinct fashion:

> If anyone would like to acquire humility, I can, I think, tell him the first step. The first step is to realise [sic] that one is proud. And a biggish step, too. At least, nothing whatever

can be done before it. If you think you are not conceited, it means you are very conceited indeed.[2]

Psychologist David Myers would probably agree, insisting that human beings suffer from a persistent self-serving bias: we tend to give ourselves more credit than we're due. In what is now a well-established body of research, most people, when asked to compare themselves to others on a variety of characteristics, consider themselves above average. Businesspeople tend to think themselves more ethical than their peers. Drivers rate themselves as more skillful, even if they've had accidents. And people in general think themselves smarter, more attractive, and less racially prejudiced.[3]

Obviously, it's impossible for everyone to be above average. I suspect, though, that if I were a participant in such a study and the researchers told me the findings, I would be tempted to think, *Well, of course people think they're better than average. That's how people are! But me? I really am above average.*

Pride seems to be the way we're bent. But as I suggested in the previous chapter, there is such a thing as *appropriate* pride. Consider, for example, the way the apostle Paul talks about bragging or boasting in his letters to the church in Corinth. The believers there had a tendency to pat themselves on the back for anything that they thought marked them as being more spiritual than someone else. At one point, Paul describes them using a word that suggests having one's chest puffed up with pride (1 Corinthians 5:2)—today, we might say that they were "full of themselves."

Paul had to remind them that God chose what in the eyes of the world was foolish, weak, and low-class so that "no human being can brag in God's presence" (1 Corinthians 1:27-29). But in a later letter, Paul uses the same word, "bragging," to positively describe both their pride in him and his pride in them (2 Corinthians 1:14; 5:12; 7:4; 8:24)—and even his pride in his own actions (11:10).[4]

That's because on the one hand, there is an arrogant and self-focused kind of pride, in which one says, "I'm better than you"—a pride that took several forms in the Corinthian church. But on the other hand, there is also a kind of pride that honors God, as when Paul says, "The one who brags should brag in the Lord" (1 Corinthians 1:31).

Paul rightly takes pride in anything that shows the progress of the gospel, ultimately giving God the glory. He may have had this verse from the prophet Jeremiah in mind as he wrote:

> The LORD proclaims: the learned should not boast of their knowledge, nor warriors boast of their might, nor the rich boast of their wealth. No, those who boast should boast in this: that they understand and know me. I am the LORD who acts with kindness, justice, and righteousness in the world, and I delight in these things, declares the LORD.
>
> –Jeremiah 9:23-24

In other words, it's right to take pleasure in anything we do that promotes justice and flourishing. The question is whether the pleasure comes from feeling special or morally superior to someone else, or from experiencing a taste of hope and wholeness from being part of God's work of peacemaking. This, in essence, is our happiness, our blessedness: we were meant to glory in God's shalom.

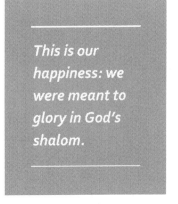

This is our happiness: we were meant to glory in God's shalom.

For me, as a minister and marriage educator, for example, I glimpse shalom when spouses lay down their defenses and turn toward one another in openness, reaching out to connect and understand. I hope, of course, that this is an experience of shalom—the balm of relational peace—for them too.

In those moments, I must confess, I am tempted to professional pride, to nurture the thought, "Hey, I'm really good at this," in a way that makes it all about me. But let me be clear. It would be false humility to act as if I had done nothing, to pretend with exaggerated modesty that I had no knowledge or skill to contribute to the process. If that were truly the case, then it would be useless for me to spend all the hours I do in training others, or even writing books like these, in which I hope to influence your attitudes and behaviors.

Moreover, the divine humility we discussed in chapter 5 doesn't mean that God is modest or self-effacing. It's not as if the resurrected Jesus would walk around blushing and saying, "That whole cross thing? Aw, shucks, it was nothing."

Proper humility is the flip side of appropriate pride: let the one who brags, brag in the Lord. It's not *all* about you, as if you had the power to save the world on your own—but the stunning truth is that God has deliberately chosen to do his saving, peacemaking work in and through you, through me, through everyone who follows the path of his kingdom.

If that's not cause for joyful "boasting," what is?

Thus, we must leave space for a more subtle understanding of pride and humility in marriage that doesn't default to black-and-white stereotypes. The humility we need is not mere modesty, but a kind of self-forgetfulness.

We can turn again to C. S. Lewis, who makes the point humorously in *The Screwtape Letters*, a fictional correspondence between Screwtape, a senior-level demon experienced in the art of temptation, and his nephew Wormwood. Screwtape advises the junior tempter on how to help his human "patient" avoid the nasty virtue of humility:

> You must therefore conceal from the patient the true end of Humility. Let him think of it not as self-forgetfulness but as a certain kind of opinion (namely, a low opinion) of his own talents and character. …Fix in his mind the idea that humility consists in trying to believe those talents to be less valuable than he believes them to be. …The great thing is to make him value an opinion for some quality other than truth, thus introducing an element of dishonesty and make-believe into the heart of what otherwise threatens to become a virtue.

> By this method thousands of humans have been brought to think that humility means pretty women trying to believe they are ugly and clever men trying to believe they are fools.[5]

True humility, as Lewis suggests, involves a lack of self-concern. Ironically, the false humility of trying to pretend you're something you're not is actually a form of religious pride, a hunger to have others praise you for conspicuous virtue.

But therein lies the difficulty. Self-concern is the enemy of self-forgetfulness, and realistically, many if not most of us are a bundle of self-concern. Every single one of us enters marriage with a history of previous relationships that have shaped how we understand ourselves and others, including what we expect, want, and need from our spouses. When we don't get it, our pride may be injured, as if our emotions were to shout, "You can't do that to me!" As a result, we go on the defensive, perhaps even retaliating in revenge, and the relationship suffers.

The commitment to making peace doesn't mean that defensive pride will simply vanish by an act of will; we can't make it go away by telling ourselves that Christians shouldn't feel that way.[6] But the alternative is to actively choose the way of humility, even when we feel hurt or offended, by choosing what is best for our spouses and best for the marriage itself.

Taking Care of "Us"

As psychologist Everett Worthington has written, "Humility doesn't shout its characteristics. It is the quiet virtue."[7] In part, that's because it begins internally, with a fundamental shift in attitude. Whatever changes we make in our behaviors, an attitude of humility comes first, even if it's as simple as knowing we need to change and committing ourselves to doing so.

This may sound obvious, but one important aspect of humility begins with the recognition that you're not the only person in the marriage. As my colleague Terry Hargrave has written, "For [marriage strengthening] techniques to take root, partners must have recommitted themselves to the 'us' of their relationship."[8] He explains what he means by "us":

> "Us" is created by two individuals in a committed relationship; it takes on a personality with characteristics of its own. It is not just two individuals who share, it is two individuals who give up part of themselves to create a oneness, an "us." ...It transcends each person in the relationship, but depends on the individuals to keep it alive. ...The real heart of what makes a marriage satisfying and happy is a strong and vital "us."[9]

Here's a simple and homely example. Think back to the story of Danny and Celia in chapter 1. Though they were very much in love when they married, little annoyances have begun to open fissures in their relationship. From one side, Celia wants a neat house; disorder bothers her, and she wants it taken care of as soon as possible. From the other side, it's not as if Danny insists on being a slob. He values neatness, just not as much as Celia does—and he prefers having the freedom to decide for himself when things need to be picked up.

Neither of them is purely right or wrong. But where before there were two individuals with their own desires and preferences, there is now a union in which the two must share one space and one life. It's not that the two individuals, in all their uniqueness, suddenly cease to exist—but if they live together solely *as* individuals, there will be no marriage.

Each spouse must be willing to compromise "what I want" for "what's best for us."

Somehow, Danny and Celia must make the transition out of merely defending their competing opinions and understandings. "This is how *I* do things," must gradually give way to

"This is how *we* do things." Each must be willing to compromise "what *I* want" right now, for the sake of doing "what's best for *us*" over the long haul. It will, naturally, *feel* like a sacrifice, especially at first. But such is the nature of humility: the willingness of the individuals to sacrifice for the greater good of the relationship.

That might not sound like much fun. It's easy to exaggerate the language of Christian sacrifice in a way that paints a gloomy picture of marriage as a life of endless suffering for Jesus. But for the most part, that's not the way it works. When spouses act in humility toward one another, it builds trust and closeness, creating more freedom and a deeper and richer bond.

When Celia tells Danny to *Puh-leeeze!* pick up his socks, for example, he bristles at her tone of voice. It sounds like nagging, and he doesn't like it. He once even said to her, "If seeing my socks lying there bothers you so much, then don't look."

It seemed like an obvious and logical thing to say at the time. Not surprisingly, though, that not-so-humble response didn't do much to make peace.

This morning, however, as Danny swings his feet over the side of the bed and sees his socks lying there, a new thought occurs to him: "So what really *is* the big deal about my picking them up and putting them in the hamper? I'm going that way anyway."

Celia's made that argument a hundred times, but he's never made it far enough past his defensive response to her so-called nagging to listen openly. He knows that he has no particular personal need to do this; he'd be just fine leaving the socks lying there until they actually got in his way. "But it would make her happy, and that's good for her and good for us," Danny shrugs mentally. "I guess that's reason enough."

He reaches down, picks them up, and plods to the hamper.

Of course, whatever good might come out of that one small sacrifice would be obliterated if he were to make a self-centered fuss over it: "Look—I picked up the stupid socks! Okay? Are you happy now?" Such an outburst would leave her feeling misunderstood and alone, because it isn't just about the socks: it's about love, respect, and acceptance. It's about having Danny communicate to her, in word, deed, or both, "In all honesty, Cee, I just don't get the sock thing. But it's obviously important to you. So because I love you, I'll do something about it—because *you're* important to me."

At this point, some might ask, "Does that mean Danny's now opening himself up for a barrage of new demands, and that he has to do whatever Celia tells him?"

The question is understandable in the context of a marriage in which spouses have learned to distrust each other. Yes, he's opening himself up. Yes, it's possible that Celia will selfishly take advantage of him. Even if not, there's no guarantee that she will even respond positively. For Danny to choose humility means to act out of love for her and concern for the relationship, to do the right thing even if it involves some risk.

It may take time, but if there is any fragment of love and trust left in the marriage, Danny's small acts of selflessness will begin to strengthen both his and Celia's sense of "us." And in all likelihood, she will respond by becoming *more* flexible, not less.

For example, if Danny begins to habitually put his socks in the hamper without being asked, it will matter much less to Celia if once in a while he neglects to do so; she may either leave them there or pick them up herself without complaint. Why? Because the behavior no longer screams to her of Danny's stubbornness or slovenliness. Instead, she is more likely to take it as a sign that her husband means well but sometimes forgets.

What might humility look like from Celia's side? Here are a few possibilities. She might ask herself how important her need for a tidy house really is to the *relationship*, not just to her personally. She can consider where there would be room for a reasonable compromise. As we'll see in the next chapter, she can take the extra step of compassion, and try to see herself through Danny's eyes: even if she believes her request to be perfectly reasonable, is she asking in a way that unnecessarily puts him on the defensive?

And so on. If you identify with their story at all, or one like it, I'm sure you have your own suggestions. But whatever practical form humility might take, what comes first is a shift in perspective: we must see beyond our individual needs to the needs of the relationship. It's not all about me, and it's not all about you: it's about recognizing and nurturing "us."

꩟꩜

We do not come to marriage as blank slates. We have wants, needs, and preferences of which we are often unaware. Or, if we are aware of them, they may seem perfectly obvious and reasonable to us, as if any sane person would want the same thing or behave the same way. And we're mystified or annoyed when our spouses "don't get it." We think to ourselves, uncharitably, *Could it be that I married someone that clueless?* Or, *Is she doing this on purpose just to get back at me for something?*

When we find ourselves sliding into resentment, hostility, contempt, defensiveness and the like, we have a choice. We can act as if it's all our spouse's problem and take the attitude, implicitly or explicitly, that our way of thinking and being is the only right and decent way.

Or we can remember the divine humility of the unjustly crucified Son of God, and choose whatever small step of humility is within our power. We can choose not just what seems to be in our own best interest, but whatever is in the best interest of our spouse and of our marriage, of "us."

That's the path of peace.

The Many Expressions of Humility

We therefore have ample spiritual reasons for learning humility as followers of Christ. As an added bonus, recent research has also begun to demonstrate the social value of humility, a topic which for many years was neglected by researchers.[10] In part, that's because even if humility as a virtue is easy enough to understand philosophically, it's difficult to study scientifically. How do you measure it? Is it even appropriate to ask people to rate their own humility?[11]

Nevertheless, even when taken with a grain of salt, the results of a growing number of studies are encouraging. Researchers have found, for example, that people who are more humble:

- are more generous with their money and more inclined to show kindness to others;[12]
- are more generous in volunteering time to help others;[13]
- are more likely to respond with gratitude and trust to the kindness of others;[14]
- report stronger and happier relationships.[15]

On the other side, people who are less modest and more self-focused tend to be more aggressive, quicker to take offense and become angry, and less forgiving.[16]

Studies like these are instructive, because they help us to get at the practical expressions of humility in everyday life. Psychologist Julie Exline, for example, has defined humility as "a nondefensive willingness to see the self accurately, including strengths and limitations."[17] There again is the idea that our defensiveness can get in the way. In a similar vein, but with greater detail, June Tangney has described six broad elements of humility:

- You have an accurate (not low) view of what you can do and what you've accomplished;
- You can keep such things in proper perspective, including being able to see yourself as only one part of a bigger picture;
- You're not self-focused, that is, not preoccupied with your own concerns;
- You can admit your mistakes, weaknesses, and what you don't know;
- You're open to ideas and advice;

- You appreciate the value and contributions of others.[18]

Some of this—particularly the first three points on the list—should sound familiar. Humility is neither self-deprecation nor false modesty. It's not having a *low* opinion of oneself, but an *accurate* one.

For Christians, that means seeing ourselves and others as God does. Being humble, therefore, doesn't mean denying your abilities, but keeping those abilities in perspective. I'm reminded, for example, of Paul's words to the church in Rome:

> Because of the grace that God gave me, I can say to each one of you: don't think of yourself more highly than you ought to think. Instead, be reasonable since God has measured out a portion of faith to each one of you. We have many parts in one body, but the parts don't all have the same function. In the same way, though there are many of us, we are one body in Christ, and individually we belong to each other.
>
> –Romans 12:3-5

He's writing to a church that has struggled with ethnic tension between Jews and Gentiles, trying to figure out what it meant to be a church, together. On the one hand, the Jews considered themselves to be the *real* people of God, but found themselves in the persecuted minority. On the other, the Gentiles dared to believe themselves to be God's new favorites, especially after the Jews were expelled from Rome by Emperor Claudius (Acts 18:2).

Paul's word to both was *not* "think of yourselves as dirt," but "don't think of yourselves more highly than you ought" or "don't think that you're better than anyone else" (Romans 12:16). *You belong to each other*, he insists, *like the different parts of one body*.

Humble Christians work at seeing things from God's point of view, trying to understand their place in what he's doing. It's not so they can congratulate themselves on having the showiest and most important roles. Rather, it's because their deepest desire as peacemakers is to help accomplish the good that God intends for his people and all of creation. They have an outward-directed vision that frees them from self-concern. Simply put, when you learn to see the world as God does, you realize that it doesn't revolve around you.

☙❧

For most of us, I would imagine, Tangney's list better describes the humility to which we aspire than the humility we actually have. It's all well and good to say that humble people are not self-focused, but again, all of us have defensive reactions from time to time, of different types and varying degrees. Humility is not a once-and-done achievement, but a moment to moment journey of obedience by those who follow in the steps of a crucified Lord.

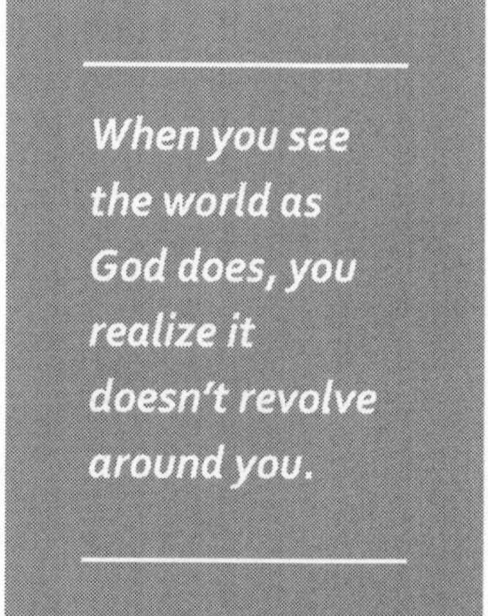
When you see the world as God does, you realize it doesn't revolve around you.

It helps to have signposts along the way. Fortunately, the last three points on Tangney's list can provide couples with just such practical guidance, so the remainder of the chapter will draw out the implications of each.

Know and admit your mistakes and limitations. "Happy are people who grieve," Jesus declared in the second Beatitude, "because they will be made glad" (Matthew 5:4).

In our day, the language of grief and mourning is often used in a narrow sense, to refer to people who are bereaved because of the loss of a loved one through death. As we saw in chapter 1, however, Jesus' statement is meant more broadly to echo the prophet Isaiah, who was offering divine words of comfort to God's people as they languished in exile.

It's true that their grief was tied to a deep sense of loss. But their sorrow was of a different kind than most of us have known: it was the loss of their land and inheritance, their identity and status, that they mourned. And importantly, their grief also contained an element of repentance. They realized too late the disobedient pride that resulted in their captivity. If they could have taken it all back, they would have.

Humble people, therefore, are aware of their sin. But in light of our defensive tendencies, we need to be careful with what comes next. It's not necessarily humble to go around saying, "I'm just a terrible, awful person."[19]

There are two reasons for this. First, haven't you ever played the part of the repentant sinner just to get people to say, "Don't be so hard on yourself. I think you're pretty terrific," or, "Wow, you must be pretty humble to say that"? Not sure of your motives? Imagine that you've just confessed your worthlessness to someone else, and he or she responds, "You're absolutely right. You *are* pretty terrible." How do you feel? Haven't they pricked your pride, just a little?

Second, the more deeply we are aware of our sin, the more deeply we must embrace the reality of grace. The two go hand in hand. It's true that the more we understand the holiness of God, the more horrifying our sin will seem to us. But to wallow in guilt, ironically, is in effect to refuse the mercy we've already been given, the forgiveness that was purchased at such enormous cost.

God has called us to be holy and is making us holy, because he himself is holy (e.g., 1 Peter 1:15-16). To dwell one-sidedly on our sin, to ignore the sanctifying work of the Holy Spirit in our lives, is not humble. It's tantamount to idolatry—because in so doing, we set our condemning word of self-judgment above God's word of grace.

The humility that leads toward peace, therefore, entails both a keen awareness of our own sin *and* a matching acceptance of God's grace. In the absence of grace, it is much harder to honestly admit we've been wrong, *with* appropriate regret and *without* defensiveness.

What do we do when our marriages are troubled? We may be absolutely sure we're in the right. We may be certain that we have no reason for repentance; we may "know" that our spouses are the ones in the wrong. But we can still pray in humility to the God who knows us better than we know ourselves:

> LORD, you have examined me. You know me. You know when I sit down and when I stand up. Even from far away, you comprehend my plans. You study my traveling and resting. You are thoroughly familiar with all my ways. There isn't a word on my tongue, LORD, that you don't already know completely. You surround me—front and back. You put your hand on me. That kind of knowledge is too much for me; it's so high above me that I can't fathom it. ...Examine me, God! Look at my heart! Put me to the test! Know my anxious thoughts! Look to see if there is any idolatrous way in me, then lead me on the eternal path!
>
> –Psalm 139:1-6, 23-24

I can't help but wonder how many marital conflicts between Christians continue to drag on and on because one or both partners are unwilling to responsibly repent of the peace-violating part they've played. It's not that we're entirely blind to our own sin. But, as described in chapter 3, we humans have a persistent self-serving habit of perception called an attribution bias. We interpret our spouse's bad behavior as a personal fault or a defect in their character. Our own behavior, however, we justify as an understandable response to his or her provocation: *I know I overreacted—but really, what was I supposed to do?*

If in humility we pray to God to examine our hearts, the Holy Spirit may reveal our own faults to us. Our job at that point is to confess, repent, and receive anew the cleansing and liberating forgiveness of God (1 John 1:9).

That's not to say that everything is our fault, or that our spouses have done nothing blameworthy, or that it's inappropriate to ask our spouses for a change of behavior. But trust me: that conversation will go much better if approached with true and demonstrated humility.

Listen humbly and openly. As I mentioned in the introduction, I've taught communication skills to hundreds of couples. One important skill is for spouses to learn to speak in ways that are more likely to be heard and received.[20] It helps, for example, to avoid saying things like "You never…" or "You always…," which are almost certain to get a defensive reaction. But I believe listening is the more fundamental skill—because if everyone learned to listen with humility and patience, it would matter much less how carefully people chose their words.

As suggested in an earlier chapter, when our partners speak, we respond first to what we *think* they said—and that may not be the same as what they meant or actually said. We actively interpret what they say, and misunderstand far more often than we care to admit. The script is repeated again and again from one home to the next. For example:

He, frowning:	"What are you so mad about?"
She, resentfully:	"Because you said ___."
He, surprised:	"I never said that."
She, insistent:	"Yes, you did."
He, now exasperated:	"No, I *didn't*."
She, vehement:	"Oh, yes, you *did*."

Around and around it goes, each spouse becoming more and more firmly convinced that the other is lying or deluded.

How does a couple get off this mad merry-go-round? At least one of the spouses needs to show enough humility to (1) stop trying to correct the other person, (2) admit he or she may have gotten it wrong, and (3) listen attentively until he or she gets it right and the other spouse feels heard.

After all, there are many reasons why we mishear and misinterpret, without realizing that we're doing so (not counting getting a little deaf, like me!):

- We're distracted and not paying full attention;
- Our mood is coloring how we interpret what our spouses are saying;
- We hear what we expect to hear;
- We react negatively because our spouse says something

> or says it in a way that would not have been acceptable in the family we grew up in.[21]

Knowing our fallibility, listening in the midst of conflict can be a powerful practical expression of humility. In workshops, I have seen some couples quickly cut through old impasses with even the most rudimentary of listening exercises, in which one spouse speaks and the other listens silently, with nothing more than the occasional nod or short comment like, "Wow!" or "I see."[22] In other words, you don't have to believe that you're wrong; but you do have to acknowledge that you *could* be, focus your attention on what your spouse is saying, and open yourself to hearing something new.

Listening, however, isn't just something we do when there's a disagreement. When Tangney suggests that the humble are open to new ideas and advice, I am reminded of Proverbs 13:10: "The empty-headed cause conflict out of pride; those who take advice are wise." Part of recognizing our limitations is to admit that we don't know everything, and sometimes need the help and wisdom of others. The problem is, as Andrew Butcher has written, it's sometimes easier to serve others than it is to be served:

> Receiving service from others is an acknowledgement of our vulnerability and of our limitations. It speaks to our inability to look after ourselves. I am vulnerable when you serve me, because I cannot hide behind what I do and because you can see who I really am: someone in need of help.[23]

This may be particularly true for husbands, who as men have been taught to base their sense of self-worth on their independence and competence. As John Gottman has found in his research, one of the consistent differences between successful and unsuccessful couples was that in successful marriages, husbands listened to and allowed themselves to be influenced by what their wives said. That doesn't mean that wives don't have to listen to their husbands! It means, rather, that wives usually accepted their husbands' influence anyway, in both kinds of couples.[24] It was the husbands' behavior that made the difference.

Men, are you listening?

Be appreciative and grateful. If in humility we are able to confess our sins and admit our limitations, if we are open to listening to and learning from each other, then the final recommendation becomes more obvious. Marriage is not something we do alone; there is an "us." Have we lost the ability to both experience and express gratitude for what we have? It's far too easy to take our marriages for granted—especially when we feel disgruntled.

One couple, for example, was at their local home improvement warehouse. The wife had a big gardening project she wanted done; the husband, apparently, was of the opinion that he had much better things to do. He sullenly pushed around the heavily laden cart, resenting each and every plant she added to the growing collection.

When they finally came to the checkout line, they stood behind a friend of mine, who later told me their story. The husband, looking for a little male sympathy, began to complain about his wife. He looked down at my friend's cart, with its comparatively tiny payload, and muttered enviously, "You're so lucky."

He had no way of knowing, of course, that my friend had recently and tragically lost his wife, and was in the process of rebuilding a life without her. *Lucky?* he thought to himself, as he wondered what to say in return. *Buddy, let me tell you how "lucky" I am. I would do anything to have my wife back; I'd happily plant that whole cart of flowers ten times over.*

A word, therefore, to the wise: cultivate gratitude. Look for the things you can appreciate about your spouse, and tell him or her. But make sure to do so without sneaking in any qualifications like, "But what I would *really* appreciate is..." or "Next time, you could do better by..." These come across like criticism and invalidate all the good that simple and humble words of appreciation might do.

In short: humbly take care of "us" while there's still an "us" to take care of.

⁂

Humility is a foundational virtue that in turn is grounded in the story of God's work of peace. As Caroline Simon has suggested, in order to know who we truly are in God's eyes, in order to avoid self-deception, we need to cultivate the following "correctives to pride":

> the faith that allows us to face the truth about ourselves because the depth of our brokenness finds its answer in grace; the hope that, though we often wander from the path, grace will make straight what we have bent; and the love, compassion, and gratitude that follow from seeing our own and others' stories as part of God's story.[25]

The more we learn to imagine ourselves as peacemakers, the more will we be able to see ourselves as part of something much larger than the personal concerns that drive much of our marital interaction. That humbling perspective must find practical expression in our marriages, as we learn to see each other as God does: people who, despite their brokenness, are of unspeakable value and called to be ambassadors for peace.

Those who are wise humble themselves before God. And the wise who are married embody that humility at home.

⁂

Questions for discussion and reflection:

1. Think back to the story at the beginning of the chapter: "Don't you think that's enough salt?" Remember a time in which you took offense at something your spouse said, that may not have been meant as an insult. What happened? What part of your pride was insulted? Where else do you see the negative effects of pride in your marriage or other relationships?

2. Can you remember a time when you were at your wit's end and cried out to God? What was it like to feel so dependent on him? Do you identify at all with Moses' warning in Deuteronomy 6, that we should be careful not to forget God when we get comfortable? If so, how?

3. Again, recall the story of Danny and Celia. The behaviors and attitudes they brought with them into the marriage can sometimes bring them into conflict. In what way, if at all, do you see something similar in your own marriage? In the story, Danny makes a choice to do something different, not for his own sake, but simply because it would make Celia happy and would be good for the "us" of their marriage. What would it look like for you to make a similar choice in your own home?

4. Think of something you've done or said in your marriage that you regret. Be as objective and realistic as possible; try to imagine the situation as God might see it. What did you do that violated peace? How deeply and honestly have you been willing to take responsibility for it before God? Before your spouse?

5. Would you say that your spouse is a good listener? What does he or she do that leads you to say that? What about you—how well do you think you listen to your spouse? Think back to your last disagreement. Did you feel understood, even if you still differed at the end of the conversation? What would the two of you need to do differently for both of you to feel understood, especially in the midst of conflict?[26]

6. When you first got married, there were probably things you admired about your spouse: personal characteristics and qualities for which you were grateful. Over time, you may have forgotten some of them—or you may have discovered others! If you were to brag about your spouse to someone else now, what would you say? Tell your spouse what you appreciate about him or her,

without any "buts" or qualifications. If you can think of one, tell a story to illustrate what you're talking about.

7

THE COMPASSION CONNECTION

In the last two chapters, I've offered a biblical perspective on the virtue of humility and its practical application to marriage. Humility in marriage is more than modesty. It's a kind of self-forgetfulness in which we are able to set aside our defensiveness—even if only temporarily!—to focus on what is good for our spouse or our relationship. But do we understand what our spouses need? Are we moved to do something about it? In the next two chapters, we'll look at the virtue of compassion, beginning with the crucial role of empathy in building a strong marriage.

ഇര

Half a century ago, the moral imagination of Americans was riveted by a New York *Times* headline: "37 Who Saw Murder Didn't Call the Police."

It was March of 1964. During the cold, dark early morning hours of Friday the 13th, 28-year-old Kitty Genovese was coming home from work. As she walked from her car to her apartment, an assailant caught and stabbed her. The newspaper article alleged that dozens of people saw Genovese as she was attacked not once, but three times; she was stabbed repeatedly and then raped as she lay dying. They heard her screams and came to their windows to see what was happening.

But no one, supposedly, alerted the police.

The story quickly gained notoriety. At one level, it was taken as a cautionary tale of mental illness, urban violence and unrest. But at another level, it became a parable of What's Wrong With the World These Days. *Nobody seems to care anymore about what happens to their neighbors,* pundits mused. *Are people so scared, self-centered, or apathetic that they won't lift a finger to help a woman who is being brutalized right in front of them?*

The *Times* article, unfortunately, was somewhat inaccurate, skewed by an editor who wanted to play up the apathy angle. It's true that some witnesses decided not to get involved. One man, for example, saw the crime from across the street and did nothing to help; instead, he took a nap.

But the facts seem to be these. Only a small number of people could actually see the attacks. During the first, the assailant was scared off by a man who yelled at him to leave Genovese alone. When the murderer returned, his second attack (there was no third) was in a place where it couldn't be seen. Even so, people did call for help. When emergency personnel arrived, they found Genovese cradled in the arms of a Good Samaritan named Sophia Farrar who had risked leaving her apartment to care for her as she died.[1]

Still, the *Times* version of the Genovese story generated much hand-wringing speculation as to how something like this could happen. A whole tradition of psychological research followed. The case appears in many introductory psychology textbooks as an illustration of a well-established phenomenon known as the *bystander effect.* If you see somebody suffering or being victimized, will you reach out to help? The research says, "It depends."

If you're one of many in a crowd, you're much less likely to get involved. This is the principle of *diffusion of responsibility:* it's as if everyone is waiting for someone *else* to be the first to take action before jumping in. And, tellingly, it depends on whether the victim is part of a social group with which you identify; how the person is dressed, for example, can make all the difference.[2]

We'd like to believe that if we needed help, someone would come to our aid. We'd like to believe that if others needed our help, we would give it. And both do happen. But we also have reasons for *not* helping. Or taking a risk. Or getting involved. Basically, we have our reasons for not extending compassion to strangers.

Would we do better in our homes, with the people whom we supposedly love?

If our children fell, we'd help them up and bandage their scraped knees. If our spouses were the victims of crime or illness, we'd do whatever we could to care for their needs.

But what if our spouses were hurt or suffering—whether we think with good reason or not—because of something *we* said or did? Would we still want to help? Or would defensiveness and self-interest get in the way?

Just as the life of Jesus reveals to us God's essential humility, so too does it demonstrate the compassion that grows from that humility. If we are to be peacemakers in our marriages, we must learn to follow the teaching and example of Jesus in both virtues.

And just in case we need a lesson in compassion, he has a story to tell, of the original Good Samaritan (Luke 10:25-37).

The Compassion of God

Jesus and his disciples were passing through Samaria on their way to the trouble that awaited in Jerusalem. An expert in Jewish law came forward to challenge Jesus, testing him with a theological question: what must he do to gain eternal life, to have his place in the age that the Messiah would bring?

I've had a few graduate students throw down the rhetorical gauntlet over the years. One student, who had a background in philosophy, told me later that he would ask questions in class just to see if I could answer them. Eventually, satisfied with my responses, he gave up the game.

Somehow, I doubt that it would have worked for me to respond with a question of my own: "What do *you* think?" But that's exactly what Jesus did: "What is written in the Law?" he asked. "How do you interpret it?"

It was as if to say, "You're the legal expert—what's your professional opinion?" No doubt Jesus discerned the man's pride; it would have taken little to bait him into an opportunity to flaunt his knowledge. But whatever Jesus' intention, the man did in fact answer his own question, citing Deuteronomy 6:5 and Leviticus 19:18—"You must love the Lord your God with all your heart, with all your being, with all your strength, and with all your mind, and love your neighbor as yourself." It was a good answer. As a matter of fact, it was the answer Jesus himself might have given (cf. Matthew 22:34-40).

But then Jesus responded, "You have answered correctly—do this and you will live." Suddenly, the lawyer was caught in his own trap. He had thought to embarrass Jesus with a potentially controversial question. Now, *he* was embarrassed. Jesus had deftly turned the spotlight away from the man's intellectual expertise to his moral integrity: did he practice what he preached?

The clever lawyer, however, wasn't done yet. Recovering quickly, he came up with a promising maneuver to save face. "And who is my neighbor?" he asked. There was no controversy about the need for a good Jew to love God wholeheartedly. But there would have been plenty of room for debate about "neighbors."

In the Sermon on the Mount, Jesus had taught the following:

> You have heard that it was said, *You must love your neighbor and hate your enemy.* But I say to you, love your enemies and pray for those who harass you so that you will be acting as children of your Father who is in heaven. –Matthew 5:43-45

Nowhere in Scripture were God's people instructed directly to hate their enemies.[3] But apparently, by Jesus' day, the command to love one's neighbors had taken on some extra baggage. Some Jews believed it right and good to hate Gentiles for being the enemies of God. And the legal expert's question may have been particularly tricky as he and Jesus stood facing each other in the land of the Samaritans, the ethnic enemies of the Jews.

How to answer? As he did so often, Jesus responded by telling a story.

A man was traveling from Jerusalem to Jericho. It was known to be a dangerous journey, and sure enough, the unfortunate traveler was set upon by bandits who stripped and beat him, and left him near dead on the side of the road.

Would anyone stop to help?

In turn, two Jews, a priest and a Levite, came down the road, perhaps returning from their duties at the Jerusalem temple. Each had the same response. When they saw the body, they crossed to the other side of the road and went on their way. Why? Jesus doesn't say. All that matters to the story is that these two religious professionals refused compassion to the wounded stranger.

Then a Samaritan happened by; we might imagine the look of disgust on the legal expert's face as Jesus introduced the character. Jesus described the Samaritan as seeing the injured man and being filled with *compassion*, in stark contrast to the priest and Levite. The word used in Luke's account literally means that the Samaritan had a deeply emotional "gut reaction" to the man's plight, and acted accordingly.[4]

The Samaritan dressed the stranger's wounds, then hoisted him up onto his own donkey. In so doing, he was putting himself at considerable risk, since he would now have to make the rest of the dangerous journey on foot. Who knew if bandits were still about?

And making an even further sacrifice, the Samaritan took the man to an inn, and paid his tab in advance. "Take care of him," he told the innkeeper, "and when I return, I will pay you back for any additional costs." Talk about giving someone a blank check: how prudent could it have been for a Samaritan to say such a thing anywhere within shouting distance of Jerusalem?[5]

Jesus then turned to his challenger and once again asked his opinion: "What do you think? Which one of these three was a neighbor to the man who encountered thieves?" At first, the lawyer had smugly asked, "What must I do?" When Jesus unexpectedly turned the tables on him, he was sent scrambling for a moral loophole and changed his question to, "Who is my neighbor?"

But Jesus again closed off the lawyer's rhetorical escape. The victim in the parable was naked and nameless, stripped of identity, unidentifiable as a neighbor or non-neighbor. When it came to the matter of compassion, then, the question was no longer "Who is my neighbor?" but "Who *was* a neighbor to the man?" Who actually did what the commandment required? The priest? The Levite? Or—*gasp!*—the hated and reviled Samaritan?

I imagine the legal expert gritting his teeth as he responded to Jesus' question. Unable to even say the word "Samaritan," he answered, "The one who demonstrated mercy toward him."

Again, right answer. "Go and do likewise," was all Jesus said.

☙❧

"Happy are people who show mercy," Jesus taught (Matthew 5:7). The beatitude builds on the ones that come before it. The blessed are humble, because they recognize both the brokenness of the world and their own sin, and they long to see God put things right. Similarly, if humility involves self-forgetfulness, then mercy involves turning outward toward others with godly compassion. To do so is to participate in God's work of peace.

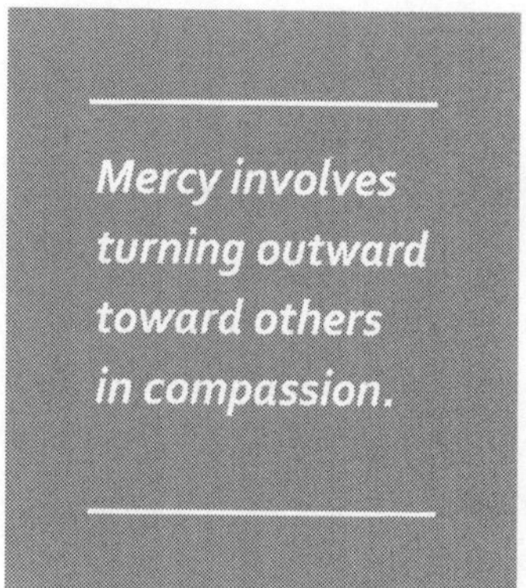
Mercy involves turning outward toward others in compassion.

The word "compassion" literally means to "suffer with" someone, to feel their pain and want to do something about it. And unlike the legal expert who challenged him, Jesus didn't just talk about neighbor-love or compassion. He demonstrated it.

Sometimes, our mental images of Jesus are too bland, as if he floated serenely above the story, devoid of strong emotion save the occasional outburst of holy indignation. But nothing could be further from the truth. It's crucial to recognize that Jesus is described repeatedly as having the same compassionate gut reaction as the Samaritan. As Henri Nouwen and his colleagues have written:

> We would misunderstand the many miraculous stories in the Gospels if we were to be impressed simply by the fact that sick and tormented people were suddenly liberated from their pains. If this were indeed the central event of these stories, a cynic might rightly remark that most people during Jesus' day were not cured and that those who were cured only made it worse for those who were not. What is important here is not the cure of the sick, but the deep compassion that moved Jesus to these cures.[6]

Jesus' compassion meant taking pity on a widow whose only son had died, telling her not to cry and raising him from the dead (Luke 7:11-15). He was moved by the predicament of the crowds that came for healing (Matthew 9:36; 14:14; 20:34), even when he was trying to get some rest (Mark 6:34). He was even concerned when they didn't have enough to eat (Matthew 15:32; Mark 8:2).

As Nouwen rightly suggests, the healing ministry of Jesus was not an end in itself. Many who encountered Jesus were neither healed nor saved. Instead, each life-saving, disease-defying miracle was a concrete demonstration of the truth of the bigger story Jesus proclaimed: "Here comes the kingdom of heaven!" (Matthew 4:17).

This doesn't mean that Jesus only did miracles as visual aids for his teaching. He had true compassion for the sick, the lame and the leprous, the blind, the deaf, and the demon-possessed. And in that heartfelt reaction to the many faces of human suffering, Jesus revealed the character of God.

Indeed, it's the God figure in some of Jesus' parables who is described as having a compassionate gut response. One story portrays God as a king who takes pity on a prostrate servant, forgiving his debt (Matthew 18:27). Another gives us God as a human father who lovingly embraces the son who spurned him and ran off to squander his inheritance (Luke 15:20).

God is spirit (John 4:24), so it would push the envelope too far to talk about the "guts" of God! But we shouldn't dismiss this as mere metaphor. Jesus himself was the embodiment of God, eternal Word made flesh (John 1:14), whose name was Emmanuel, "God with us" (Matthew 1:23).

Think about it. God. With. Us.

If we can imagine an essentially humble God, can we also imagine a compassionate one? Instead of picturing God as judging humanity disdainfully from on high, can we imagine a Father who is somehow moved by the plight of our sin and lostness? A God who is with us in our weakness and vulnerability?

This isn't some "touchy-feely" kind of theology. To understand God in this way is not to compromise a robust respect for his holiness. Quite the contrary: we must give compassion and mercy their proper due as expressions *of* his holiness. The writers of the Old Testament already knew this, and praised God for it. The psalmist, for example, declares this: "You, my Lord, are a God of compassion and mercy; you are very patient and full of faithful love" (Psalm 86:15). And this: "God is famous for his wondrous works. The LORD is full of mercy and compassion" (Psalm 111:4).[7]

Peacemakers, therefore, must be compassionate people. They willingly serve God by being conduits of peace to those who need it. And they do this because they have a larger vision of their true blessedness as humans created in the image of a compassionate God, and as ambassadors of his kingdom.

Again, even positive psychologists would make a similar point. Sonja Lyubomirsky, for example, quotes what is supposedly an old Chinese proverb:

> If you want happiness for an hour, take a nap.
> If you want happiness for a day, go fishing.
> If you want happiness for a month, get married.
> If you want happiness for a year, inherit a fortune.
> If you want happiness for a lifetime, help somebody else.[8]

That middle line is both humorous and disturbing: I'd hope for better than a month as far as marriage is concerned! But as we've already seen, even the giddy joy of a wedding is only temporary; soon, our overall happiness returns to baseline. As both the proverb and the psychological research suggest, a life of lasting contentment is not found in the pursuit of pleasant circumstances, but in the cultivation of outward-looking, other-directed virtue.

For the sake of our present discussion, the question is this: can the person we help, at least sometimes, be our spouse? And if so, what would it mean in practical terms to embody Christian compassion at home?

I will propose two broad answers. In this chapter we'll look at the role of empathy, while in the next chapter we'll consider the matter of forgiveness. But before taking the next step forward, we need to take a brief step back, to refresh the connection between compassion and the other virtues of hope, humility, and hunger.

Cracked Pots

As I write these words, I can feel the stiffness and soreness in my lower back from the household chores I did yesterday. At the same time, I am trying to push through the mental haze that has plagued me since being diagnosed with a chronic viral infection four years ago. Today, I'm foggier than usual, because I didn't sleep well last night, kept awake by an irregular heartbeat for which I will see my cardiologist this morning. And oh yes, I need a hearing aid—but am too cheap to buy one. I figure if I wait a little longer, people will get annoyed enough to take up a collection.

Even with all of this, I know I'm doing much better physically than many of my friends, relatives, and colleagues, who are suffering far worse indignities. That's what life can be like in these amazing but fragile (and aging) bodies of ours.

As much as we might prefer it, being recruited to God's kingdom work doesn't turn us into physical or moral superheroes. All of us, regardless of age, have wondrous God-given talents and abilities—

but we are still weak, fallible, broken people. We still sin against each other. We still bear the scars of the past, picking our way through the present toward a future we can't control.

And we still die.

The inescapable truth of our existence is that while we are spiritual beings, we are also creatures of flesh and blood, and there is no clear dividing line between the two.

That's not to say, as some non-biblical perspectives would have it, that the spiritual is "good" and the physical is "bad." Far from it: bodily existence is part of God's good creation. Moreover, those who follow a risen Lord look forward to a resurrection in which these bodies of ours—with all their vulnerability, their physical and emotional aches and pains—will be radiantly renewed.

No, the problem is that we live bodily in a world ravaged by sin and brokenness of every kind. That is our condition.

Though we are creatures of flesh and blood in a world ravaged by sin, we can still be vessels of God's grace and glory.

Yet Christians live in hope because they know that in God's unfolding story sin and death no longer have the final word. Peacemakers can humbly face their own brokenness because they know that new life through the power of God's Spirit is a present reality, and that anything is therefore possible. We have confidence that despite our limitations, we can be vessels of God's grace and glory here and now.

Paul, for example, in a letter to the Corinthians, once described the precarious, perilous life of an apostle thus: "We were weighed down with a load of suffering that was so far beyond our strength that we were afraid we might not survive" (2 Corinthians 1:8). And yet he wrote with enthusiasm about what he had seen God do through his ministry. He spoke of hope, confidence, and glory—of light shining in the darkness, and shining in his heart.

To those words of praise, however, he added this important qualification:

> But we have this treasure in clay pots so that the awesome power belongs to God and doesn't come from us. We are experiencing all kinds of trouble, but we aren't crushed. We are confused, but we aren't depressed. We are harassed, but we aren't abandoned. We are knocked down, but we aren't knocked out.
> –2 Corinthians 4:7-9

Too many people in Corinth, it seems, questioned Paul's credentials as an apostle. How could someone so unimpressive, someone who had suffered so much, be the real deal? Wasn't religion supposed to end suffering and make a person successful? *No*, Paul insisted: *it's not about our power and strength, but God's power in our weakness.* We are merely vessels, clay pots—the most ordinary and unremarkable of containers, always fragile, sometimes chipped and cracked. All the better for God's grace to be on clear display.

This is not a book about persecution, of course, but marriage. And this is not another chapter on humility, but compassion. Riffing on Paul's metaphor, however, here's my point: as husbands and wives who seek to bring peace to our homes, we must admit to being cracked pots. We must swallow our pride and acknowledge the weakness we bring to our marriages, else we won't have much patience or compassion for each other's brokenness and frailty.

Personally, I find Paul's statement remarkable. To begin with, it's really not that difficult to admit, "I'm not perfect." Perhaps you've said it yourself. I have. It sounds humble enough.

But who would be so arrogant as to claim perfection anyway? In all honesty, acknowledging that we're not perfect can be a way of silently implying something more: "I may not be perfect, but I'm pretty darn good—maybe even better than you!—so you ought to overlook my mistakes, because everybody makes them."

I am loath to admit my weakness. Why else is it so difficult sometimes to say, "I don't know," or "I'm sorry"? Even at home, where I should be able to relax in the certainty that I am accepted and loved for who I truly am, I often turn a blind eye to my selfishness and my testy overreactions to perceived offenses. By emotional reflex, I would much rather blame my wife than take personal responsibility for the way I feel. And I know I'm not alone in this.

Jesus has shown us the way of humility and compassion, and he has called us as peacemakers to follow his example. What that means concretely, in the midst of the challenges of married life, is that we must humbly and personally confess that we are imperfect, error-prone, and sometimes just plain selfish in ways that hurt each other and the relationship. In that humility, we must embrace hope, knowing that God has destined us to be vessels of glory. And it is in that hope that the hunger to do what's right for our spouses and our marriages will flourish.

All of this, in turn, is rich soil for the cultivation of mercy, a compassionate turning of our care and attention away from ourselves to each other. Put simply, we're all a little bit cracked, and our spouses are as cracked as we are! But the question for peacemakers is whether we will consciously extend ourselves in compassion, seeking both to understand and to forgive.

Love Your ~~Enemy~~ Spouse

Helping couples prepare for marriage is one of the most enjoyable things I do. The bride and groom are filled with love and optimism; they affectionately hold hands and look directly into each other's eyes. They know that good marriages take work, and are willing to learn, trusting that they will somehow solve any problems that come their way.

What they have more difficulty imagining is the way that two people who began their relationship as lovers and best friends can become enemies.

At first, we enter married life hoping for the best. Lori Gordon, for example, has suggested that couples typically bring these three broad hopes to their budding relationship:

- everything good I have ever had, I will keep;
- everything I ever wanted but didn't have, I will find with you;
- everything that went wrong in the past, such as disappointment, betrayal, fear, misunderstanding, arguments, violence or abandonment that may have happened to me or that I have seen happen to others in my life, will not happen with you whom I trust, love, and feel loved by.

But not surprisingly, with such hopes come the related but opposing fears:

- everything good I ever had I may be losing;
- everything good I ever wanted, I may not find with you;
- everything upsetting that ever happened to me is about to or will happen again with you.[9]

In other words, we bring emotional expectations to the relationship; we have hopes and dreams of which we may be only dimly aware. When these hopes are disappointed or dashed, when our implicit fears are realized, love and trust become much more difficult. We may know intellectually that our spouses don't mean to hurt us. But in those moments of anger or disillusionment, that's how it feels, and that's how we react.

There are good reasons for this that reach back to our earliest years. Children have a right to the loving care and attention of their parents. But in a broken world, not all receive it. Love may be given inconsistently, with strings attached, or not at all—with long term consequences for later relationships.

In recent decades, research on the inner workings of the brain has helped us to understand those consequences in greater detail.[10] The good news is that children generally learn to adapt and survive even when adults are undependable or untrustworthy. The bad news is that these survival mechanisms can make marital love and trust a rather complicated affair.

As children, we learn about the world, about what's safe and what isn't. Our developing emotions help protect us by warning us away from threatening situations. My wife and I, for example, have polar opposite responses to dogs. I like to play with them, because I think of them as affectionate pets. But where she grew up, dogs were wild and dangerous animals that traveled in packs. In such a setting, fear made complete sense as an automatic survival response. Today, she doesn't stop to ponder, "There's a dog. Should I be afraid?" The fear comes by itself, unbidden, at the mere sight of a dog nearby.

Our canine-owning friends try to tell her, "There's nothing to be afraid of. Fido is really very sweet." But it doesn't work. Emotional memories have no "time stamp."[11] When we're in a state of alarm, we don't distinguish between feelings that made sense in the past, and those that would make sense now. In situations that remind us in some way of past pain or trauma, our bodies become awash in stress hormones. We can't help feeling that there is a clear and present danger, and that we *must* do something about it.

To add another layer of complication: dogs sense and respond to human emotions. I've had dogs bark and growl at me. And why not? I know I'm not a threat, but they don't, and need to be convinced. If I remain calm, I can usually settle them down too, at least enough to have a respectful truce.

If my wife were in the same situation, however, she would automatically be afraid. Sensing her fear, the dogs would become more anxious and snarl more menacingly, to protect themselves. That would make my wife even more afraid, and so on—a self-perpetuating cycle of negative emotion with a predictably poor outcome.

Now imagine how something similar happens regularly between spouses. It's not just dogs that set off our alarms, but people. The traces of our history with others, particularly our experiences as children, are implicitly embedded in our memory. If parents and other adults reliably understood and provided for our physical and emotional needs in the past, we will generally expect relationships in the present to be safe. But if adults were undependable or unavailable, intrusive or demanding, harsh or rejecting, then we're more likely to expect relationships today to be *un*-safe. We'll be wary and defensive, and will have difficulty trusting others.

Past experience, therefore, has taught us whom we can trust and whom we cannot. That can be a good thing: we've developed an internal alarm system that alerts us to danger, commanding us to protect ourselves by clamming up or running away or fighting back. Even if from someone else's point of view there's no cause for alarm, the sense of threat happens by reflex and is very real.

We respond to slights as if past injuries were being repeated, even if our spouses intended no such thing.

But again, there's no time stamp: we respond to perceived slights by our spouses as if past injuries were being repeated, even if our spouses intended no such thing. Moreover, depending on *how* we have been hurt by others, we may develop particular areas of oversensitivity in which our alarms go off in hair-trigger fashion.

Lori Gordon likens the process to an allergic reaction:

> Anything in our lives that has hurt us, caused us pain or disappointment or distrust can develop into an "emotional allergy." ...When our partner does something that sets off an invisible warning (ignores us when we need attention, speaks sharply or dismisses us when busy), we very often find ourselves reacting as if our partner were the enemy. And we don't treat enemies like friends or lovers. We hide, demand, capitulate, blame, avoid, ignore, distrust, threaten, attack, destroy, keep secrets, nitpick, criticize, interrogate, label and call them names.[12]

Look at that laundry list of negative behaviors in the last sentence. Do you sometimes do those things with your spouse? Does your spouse do them with you? That may signal that something in your situation is poking painfully at old wounds—yours, your spouse's, or both.

That doesn't mean, of course, that every time we get upset about something, we're merely "overreacting" or that it's just our "issue." Spouses do hurtful and blameworthy things, and sometimes, we're right to be upset. The problem, however, is that as soon as we feel victimized by our spouse's behavior, it becomes harder to recognize or repent of the part *we* may have played.

Imagine a couple embroiled in a marital spat. A third party walks into the room and asks what's happening. Both spouses might be able to recite the same sequence of behaviors: he did this; she did that.

But chances are that both would also think of themselves as the victim of the other's malice or cluelessness. Like two kids caught fighting over a toy, the attitude would be, "He/she started it!" Even if both spouses were able to admit their own negative behavior, they would probably consider that behavior justified: "I only said/did that because of what he/she said/did." And unfortunately, constructive change can't happen in a marriage when both partners believe the other has to change first.

Humility requires that we recognize and accept the fact that as "cracked pots" we bring vulnerabilities to our marriages. Because of these areas of emotional sensitivity, even innocent comments or minor offenses can trigger defensive reactions that knock the relationship off course.

The dance is a familiar one. Without necessarily meaning to, you do or say something that offends me. Feeling victimized and self-protective, I respond to you as if you were my enemy. But because you're not aware of having done anything wrong, you now feel victimized, so you react defensively. But that just confirms my suspicion that you're unable or unwilling to admit you're wrong. And on it goes, back and forth, each of us feeling righteous in our own hurt or anger while hurting or angering the other.[13]

In a sense, this is "normal" inasmuch as we all suffer the same affliction. But from a larger kingdom perspective, it's also part of the brokenness that needs divine redemption.

How should a peacemaker respond?

As we've seen in the parable of the compassionate Samaritan, Jesus radically redefined what it means to love one's neighbor. The legal expert who had challenged Jesus wanted to divide people into two camps: neighbors and enemies. He would love everyone in the first group, hate everyone else, and feel good doing so.

But Jesus cast such self-serving and worldly logic aside. Those who wish to participate in God's kingdom must love their enemies. Indeed, he pressed the point even further:

> If you love only those who love you, what reward do you have? Don't even the tax collectors do the same? And if you greet only your brothers and sisters, what more are you doing? Don't even the Gentiles do the same? Therefore, just as your heavenly Father is complete in showing love to everyone, so also you must be complete. –Matthew 5:46-48

We don't need to be told to favor our friends. But loving our enemies? That's another story.

It is, in fact, *God's* story, the story of peace spreading through a fractured world and a fractious people. In the Beatitudes, Jesus taught that those "who make peace…will be called God's children" (Matthew 5:9); in the passages above, he commanded us to love our enemies, to show that we are children of our heavenly Father. The connection isn't accidental. Do we need any more than this to be convinced that peacemakers must love their enemies?

"But wait," one might say. "Did Jesus really mean to apply this to marriages? Was he thinking about married couples when he commanded his followers to love their enemies?" Perhaps not. But such questions are too similar to the one asked by the legal expert: "Who is my neighbor?" If you want to know which of our enemies

Jesus really wants us to love, the answer is simple: love the one you don't want to love.

And sometimes, that will mean reaching out in compassion to the spouse who has just offended you.

Everyday Empathy

As with most couples, my wife and I would probably never have met and married if we hadn't already shared some things in common. We were both students at the same university, and involved in the same Christian groups. We were both among the "smart kids" rather than the "cool kids" growing up, and geekily enthusiastic about *Star Trek* and *The Lord of the Rings*.

But, of course, there were also differences. Early in our marriage, as we awoke each Saturday, she would turn to me and ask, "So, what's your plan for the day?" Immediately, my brain would go into overdrive. On the inside, I would think: *"Plan"? What plan? Who makes plans on Saturday? Is there something wrong with me? Or is there something wrong with her?* On the outside, I would simply frown with visible annoyance and say, "No plan." Then, suspecting some ulterior motive on her part, I'd add, "Why do you ask?"

The simple truth was that she already had in mind a rough schedule for her day, even if I couldn't conceive of such a thing myself. And she was checking with me to see if she needed to make adjustments.

In the evening, as we retired to bed, something similar would happen. Envisioning all the unspeakable horrors that could happen if we didn't protect ourselves properly, she would ask, "Are all the doors and windows locked?" In order to relax and go to sleep, she needed to check this item off her mental list.

But my typical first reaction was again a defensive one. I heard her request for information as if it were a criticism: "Did you remember to lock the doors? Or did you forget—you slacker?"

Over time our marital "us" grew and developed. We learned more about what made the other person tick, and learned to allow for our differences. Some things haven't changed: she still asks if the doors are locked, and for the same reasons.

But some things *have* changed. Accepting that her concern about the doors and windows is a reasonable one, I check them each night before bed—not because it's worrisome to me, but because that's what "we" do. The behavior has become so routine that I sometimes can't remember if I've done it, and have to get out of bed to find out. But now, when she asks, I no longer hear a nagging wife, but someone with a legitimate concern, asking a simple question that needs only a simple answer.

That's the give and take of marriage. I've had to learn to try to see the world through my wife's eyes, and not just my own. She, in turn, tries to see through mine. We don't always succeed. But that's how it goes with cracked pots.

Nevertheless, we're also vessels for the awesome power of God. If that power can help the apostle Paul survive floggings, imprisonment, and shipwreck, maybe it can help us take down the walls we put up between us and offer a little compassionate empathy for each other's vulnerabilities.

℘ ℘

"At its core," writes one author, "compassion is a process of connecting by identifying with another person."[14] I suspect that most of us already have the capacity for this kind of empathic connection, to feel what others feel and respond accordingly.

Even children seem capable of the basics of empathy. For example, when my daughter was less than a year old, she had learned to sit up on her own. One evening, she was sitting on our bed, playing with a wooden ruler, enjoying the sound it made as she slapped it repeatedly on the bedcovers.

I was sitting on the floor next to the bed with my head poking up, encouraging the game. Suddenly, the ruler made a wild swing—*whap!*—and caught me right in the eye. "Ow!" I yelled, grimacing and covering the injured eye with my hands.

She stopped, and sat there for a moment staring at me. Then she did something I didn't expect: bending from the waist, she leaned over and kissed my eye.

Maybe you cringed or winced yourself as you imagined the ruler hitting my eye. Or you've watched a news report as family members of a murder victim were interviewed; when tears came to their eyes and their voices broke, you felt their sorrow. Or you've been in a sports arena when a professional athlete took a vicious hit from an opposing player, and a collective gasp went up from the crowd.

Most of us are already capable of empathy; the question is whether we're willing to use it.

We don't need to learn empathy from scratch; most of us are already capable at some level of identifying with the feelings and experiences of others. And we can get better at it. The immediate question for our marriages, however, is whether we're willing to use what ability we have, particularly when we feel injured or offended by what our spouses have said or done.

The practical side of empathy needn't be complicated. As John Gottman has written,

> [Empathy] refers to attempting to listen to the partner's negative emotions with compassion and understanding and trying to see the partner's emotions through the partner's eyes. …Then they communicate empathy and validation. A good summary of this validation is being able to communicate something like: "It makes sense to me that you would have these feelings, and needs, because…"[15]

If humility is expressed through patient and open listening, then what compassion adds is the desire to understand from the inside out what our spouses are feeling. As the saying goes, we try to walk a mile—sometimes even just a few feet!—in their shoes. Then we connect with our spouses emotionally by saying something that shows that we "get it."

We want to be understood. We want at least one person in our lives who knows who we are, with our foibles and feelings, and still loves and accepts us. Our spouse should be that person for us, and we for them. If we learn to give compassion through empathy, it will not only build a sense of warmth and unity in our marriages, it will also help to repair the inevitable rifts.

Here are some suggestions to guide you further down the path.

Confess your own vulnerabilities. Having areas of sensitivity in which we sometimes overreact doesn't make us monsters. Nor does it mean that everything that goes wrong is our fault. It means that we're cracked pots.

And it means we have a choice to make, day in and day out. As suggested in the previous chapter, we must learn to take humble responsibility for the part we've played in relationship struggles.

This isn't a matter of assigning blame. How big a part our vulnerability and defensiveness has played isn't as important as the simple fact that continuing to be defensive will feed the conflict. And the more we deny our own weakness, the less acceptance or compassion we will have for our spouse's sensitivities.

We don't have to know all the reasons for our emotional allergies. That can be a long term goal of exploration in the company of a trustworthy counselor. But we must at least know that we *have* such vulnerabilities before we can confess them to ourselves, to God, and to each other.

Marital therapists and researchers Andy Christensen and Neil Jacobson have identified five common areas of vulnerability that partners bring to marriage. They express each as both a universal human need and a personal statement that captures the associated emotion.[16] Although I have framed them in terms of experiences from childhood, such allergies can stem from our history of adult relationships too.

See if any of the following resonate with you:

- *Security: "Don't ever leave me."*

  As a child, you may not have been able to count on the consistent, responsive care of your parents. As a result, you may be keenly sensitive to anything that feels like abandonment, rejection, or a lack of commitment, and may become suspicious, clingy, or demanding.
- *Freedom: "Help, I'm trapped."*

  Perhaps your parents' love felt intrusive; it was more about their need for closeness than yours. They reacted badly to any demand on your part for more space. If so, even legitimate requests for closeness from your partner may feel smothering. Sometimes, you want to run.
- *Admiration: "I am somebody."*

  Your parents may have been too wrapped up in their own concerns to applaud your accomplishments. Or they may have doled out attention and recognition unfairly between you and your siblings. You may feel slighted, therefore, if your spouse doesn't notice or praise your competence or success, and might even envy theirs.
- *Approval: "Tell me I'm okay."*

  Were your parents demanding or exacting in what they expected of you, and stingy with their approval? You may be prone to hearing criticism and disapproval in your partner's remarks, even when it's not intended. Disagreement may feel like rejection.
- *Control: "I'm in charge."*

  When you asserted your independence as a child, how did your parents respond? Did they trust you to do things yourself or let you make any of your own decisions? If not, you may often resent that your spouse seems to be trying to control you or tell you what to do.

This is not, of course, an exhaustive list. The point is to recognize what vulnerabilities you already had *before* the marriage, so you can take responsibility for them in the present. Doing so gives you more freedom to accept your partner's vulnerabilities as well.

Calm yourself. It's very difficult to give compassion to your spouse when you're actively anxious or angry. When having a difficult interaction, pay attention to your body's signals that you're getting stressed out: headache, tightness in the neck and shoulders, clammy hands, a clenched jaw, a churning stomach, and so on. Agree with each other as to when and where to return to the conversation, take a break, and do things that actually help you to relax. Then come back and try again.

Tune in and be curious. If you're reasonably calm, and know your own vulnerabilities, it's easier to tune in to your partner's feelings without being sidetracked by your own.

Mona Fishbane suggests that the proper attitude is one of humble curiosity.[17] Instead of defending your own version of what happened between you, take a step back and try to think of your spouse as the main character in his or her own story instead of the villain in yours. Do they have a story to tell about one of the vulnerabilities above, or perhaps another that's not on the list? Focus your attention and be curious. Suspend judgment and try to understand what it's like to be them, with their history and experiences.

Show that you understand. If you're able to put aside your own concerns long enough to empathize with what your spouse is feeling, it may already show in your face. But it also helps to put that understanding into words: "Wow—I had no idea you had gone through that. I think I understand now why you reacted the way you did. I did (describe the behavior) and you felt (name the emotion)."

If you have your own story to share in response, go ahead; just make sure that your purpose is to show that you understand how your spouse must feel, not to get sympathy for yourself. How do you know the difference? If you tell your story, and your spouse doesn't respond sympathetically, and you resent it, you've made it more about *getting* compassion rather than giving it.

Give empathy before encouragement. This final suggestion is for the entire Christian community. When we have compassion for others, we see their suffering and want to help. Often, we say soothing words to let people know that everything's going to be all right. Among Christians, this can take the form of reminding people that "God's in charge," or as suggested in an earlier chapter, quoting Bible verses like Jeremiah 29:11 or Romans 8:28.

The desire to be encouraging—to give people courage—is a good one. But if we're honest, we might recognize that part of our motivation is not just to help others, but to help ourselves. The suffering of others can tweak our own uncertainty; we remind them that God's in charge because we need that reassurance ourselves.

When we tell others, including our spouses, "Cheer up—just pray about it, and it'll all work out," they may not thank us for our wisdom. To be clear, I'm *not* saying that there's something wrong with the encouragement to pray or to trust God. Sometimes, that's exactly what someone needs or wants to hear.

But they're not likely to receive that counsel well if they don't think we're willing to walk with them in their pain. Even if the content of our words is "religiously correct," they'll know intuitively by *how* we say those words whether they can really count on us to be there for them. Encouragement is a valuable and necessary ministry of Christians to each other.

But sometimes, empathy comes first.

Blessed are the merciful. As peacemakers, we know the mercy we have received from a compassionate God. It comes as a gracious gift, despite our limitations, despite our vulnerabilities—and we are thereby empowered to be vessels of mercy to others, including to our spouses.

In marriage, the most basic expression of compassion is empathy. But the pursuit of peace may require us to stretch even further. If we are willing to extend empathy to our spouses, can we also forgive?

❧☙

Questions for discussion and reflection:

1. Search online for videos demonstrating the "bystander effect" (e.g., see endnote # 2 for this chapter for an excellent example posted on YouTube). What are your gut reactions to the video? How do you think you would have responded in the same situation? What, if anything, does this tell you about yourself?

2. Can you remember a time in which you were deeply moved to compassion by someone else's predicament? What was the situation, and what did you do? Can you also imagine God having deep compassion for you? If so, what personal significance does this have for you? If not, why not?

3. It's easier to see the cracks in our spouse's pot than it is to see our own. What hopes did you have for your marriage that have been disappointed? If you were to tell someone the story of that disappointment, what faults would you point to in your spouse? In yourself? Is one of you more to blame than the other? Why?

4. Consider the metaphor of emotional "allergies," and the list given by Christensen and Jacobson. Does one of these resonate with you, or can you identify and name another? Tell a story of how that allergy was triggered in a situation other than your marriage, perhaps some time in the past. If it feels safe to do so, swap stories with your spouse or discussion group. Ponder together how your vulnerabilities interact and clash when you're having an argument.

5. Have you ever had the experience of feeling like your spouse was your enemy, and then having a revelation as you saw the situation through his or her eyes? Tell the story. What changed? Did you resist the revelation or welcome it?

6. Peacemakers must love their enemies. We may not think of our spouses as "enemies," but sometimes it feels that way, particularly when the emotional sore spots we brought to marriage get irritated. What will you do to love your spouse by giving compassionate empathy for his or her vulnerabilities?

8

MERCY IS FOR GIVING

The previous chapter introduced the virtue of compassion, beginning with the story of the Good Samaritan as an example of God's mercy. Making peace in our homes requires the humility to recognize that we are "cracked pots," responsible for the vulnerabilities we bring with us to marriage. And if we hunger for what is right, we will want to extend ourselves in empathy to our spouses, striving to understand what it's like to be them. But godly mercy doesn't end there. In this chapter, we must face what for many of us are the most difficult aspects of compassion: to apologize and to forgive.

ꟸ

No couple is immune: we have all done things to offend our spouses, and we have all been offended in turn. Sometimes, the offenses are mere slights, and we may be able to shake them off without too much effort. Sometimes, it's the accumulation of slights that rankles. And as we saw in the last chapter, when we have empathy—when we understand why our spouses are behaving as they are—it can take the sting out of the offense.

But not all of it. Not always.

You may have memories of when your spouse hurt you deeply. The images come readily: the party at which you stood dumbfounded while your spouse humiliated you; the moment you discovered what was really happening on those "business trips"; the empty bottle; the raised fist. The pain of those memories lingers, often just beneath the surface.

> *If you've been the victim of injustice, God's peace has been violated.*

Empathy can give us much needed insight; it can help us recognize when we've misinterpreted, misread, or exaggerated our partner's feelings and motivations. But it's one thing to understand a behavior, and another to condone it. If you've truly been the victim of injustice, however slight, God's peace has been violated. That's no small matter. Your pain is both real and justified. You know it, and God knows it.

But here's the question: what kind of forgiveness does God demand of peacemakers? Or better yet: what kind of forgiveness does a God of peace make possible?

☙❧

Consider the story of Immaculée Ilibagiza, a young Rwandan woman who miraculously survived the slaughter of thousands of Tutsis in the spring and summer of 1994. Most of her family was executed by mobs of Hutus who had joined the government-sponsored militia; her favorite brother, for example, was betrayed, humiliated, then hacked to pieces with machetes. Some of the men who went from town to town murdering and raping had once been neighbors, friends, and even dinner guests in Immaculée's home.

She survived only by the ambivalent charity of a local pastor, who hid her together with several other women for weeks in a three by four foot bathroom. Crammed together with little light or food, wasting away from malnutrition, the women lived in terrified silence as they listened to the sound of soldiers randomly and repeatedly searching the house for more Tutsis to kill. Eventually rebel forces, composed mostly of expatriate Tutsis whose families had fled earlier persecutions, took control of the country and ended the massacre.

Not long after, Immaculée was given the singular privilege of confronting the leader of the gang that murdered her mother and brother. When the dirty and emaciated prisoner was dragged before her, she recognized him immediately: Felicien, a businessman whose children had once been her playmates.

An official named Semana shoved the stumbling and broken Felicien into the room, demanding that he explain himself to Immaculée. Here is her account:

> I wept at the sight of his suffering. Felicien had let the devil enter his heart, and the evil had ruined his life like a cancer in his soul. He was now the victim of his victims, destined to live in torment and regret. I was overwhelmed with pity for the man. ... Felicien was sobbing. I could feel his shame. He looked up at me for only a moment, but our eyes met. I reached out, touched his hands lightly, and quietly said what I'd come to say.
>
> "I forgive you."[1]

Semana was stunned and furious; he had lost four of his own six children to the slaughter, and had likely expected to get some second-hand satisfaction from Felicien's humiliation. In anger, Semana turned on her:

> "What was that all about, Immaculée? That was the man who murdered your family. I brought him to you to question...to spit on if you wanted to. But you forgave him! How could you do that? Why did you forgive him?"
>
> I answered him with the truth: "Forgiveness is all I have to offer."[2]

That spirit of forgiveness didn't come to her all in one dramatic moment of confrontation. She had already begun to cultivate it prayerfully in the dark and silence of her captivity, hiding in the pastor's bathroom. She knew that God loved even those who were seeking her life. Opening her heart, she prayed for the killers and heard God's voice: *Forgive them; they know not what they do.*[3]

And through that prayer, she began to know peace.

The words she heard, of course, are the ones spoken by Jesus from the cross (Luke 23:34), words of incomprehensible mercy toward those who betrayed, mocked, and tortured him, words of undeserved forgiveness toward the people who in their willful ignorance crucified the Lord of glory (1 Cor 2:8). It was only with much anguished prayer that Immaculée Ilibagiza was able to release her anger—a fully justified anger—to God, enabling her to faithfully follow the compassionate example of Jesus.

Such stories set before us a question we might prefer not to ask: if we claim to follow Jesus, what must *we* forgive?

Extravagant Forgiveness

In a letter to the church in Corinth, Paul insisted that those who follow the way of love don't "keep a record of complaints" (1 Cor 13:5). Many of us, unfortunately, are inveterate scorekeepers with long memories—and a story in the gospel of Matthew suggests that the apostle Peter may have been one too.

Peter approached Jesus with a question: "Lord, how many times should I forgive my brother or sister who sins against me? Should I forgive as many as seven times?" (Matthew 18:21). We're not told what prompted Peter to ask. (Did he have a fight with one of the other disciples? With his wife?)

Whatever the situation, he may have thought he was being good and generous with the number seven; after all, some rabbis taught that *three* times was sufficiently praiseworthy.[4] Watching Jesus' example, Peter had learned enough to know that he should reach higher. Surely, seven would be more than enough!

But imagine what would have happened if Jesus had said, "Yes, Peter, seven will be just fine." That answer would have sanctified the scorekeeping Peter was probably already doing, perhaps even justifying a certain slow-burning, self-righteous indignation: *Five... man, this is really hard, but I have to do what Jesus said... Six... Hang in there, Peter, just one more time and you can let him have it...*

That's why Jesus said nothing of the kind. If there was any hint of smugness in Peter's question, Jesus' response punctured it rather unceremoniously: "Not just seven times, but rather as many as seventy-seven times" (Matthew 18:22). Some translators, in fact, render the number as "seventy *times* seven," which would have upped the ante even further.

So—was Jesus telling Peter that he had to forgive 490 times? And that he was therefore free to retaliate on offense number 491?

Hardly. Jesus wasn't saying, "Nice try, Peter, but your number isn't nearly high enough." The message wasn't, "Your calculations are off," but rather, "Real forgiveness—from the heart—doesn't calculate offenses, period." And in case Peter missed the point, Jesus told a parable about the nature of forgiveness in God's kingdom (Matthew 18:23-35).

Once upon a time, there was a king with many servants, one of whom owed the king an enormous sum of money, more than he could possibly pay back, ever, even if he worked at it his entire lifetime. Following standard operating procedure, the king ordered the servant, his family, and all his possessions to be sold, with the proceeds to be applied against the debt.

But the servant threw himself to the ground and begged the king to be patient with him, promising to pay the debt back. It was an empty promise, made in desperation. To the servant's surprise, however, the king responded with extravagant mercy: moved with deep compassion, he not only let the servant go, but wiped the entire debt off the books.

You would think that someone who had just been treated with such unexpected grace would be light-hearted and full of forgiveness for others. But no. As soon as he left the king's presence, he found another servant who owed him nothing more than pocket change compared to the debt from which he had just been released. When the second servant begged his patience, the first servant refused, and threw the unfortunate debtor into prison.

News of this quickly reached the king, who was understandably incensed. He ordered the servant to be brought once again before the throne. "You wicked servant!" the king boomed. "I forgave you all that debt because you appealed to me. Shouldn't you also have mercy on your fellow servant, just as I had mercy on you?" (Matthew 18:32-33).

The king threw the unforgiving servant into prison, handing him over to the torturer. Jesus ends the story with this final, chilling word: "My heavenly Father will also do the same to you if you don't forgive your brother or sister from your heart" (Matthew 18:35).

Yikes.

That ending, however, shouldn't come as a complete surprise. Earlier in the gospel of Matthew, Jesus had taught his disciples to pray, "Forgive us for the ways we have wronged you, just as we also forgive those who have wronged us" (Matthew 6:12). The prayer assumes that those who follow Jesus are already in the habit of giving mercy to others, even as they ask to receive mercy from God. And lest the point be lost, Jesus followed the prayer immediately with this warning: "If you forgive others their sins, your heavenly Father will also forgive you. But if you don't forgive others, neither will your Father forgive your sins" (Matthew 6:14-15).

Here we must drive a theological stake into the ground: Jesus is *not* setting up a system of religious works in which we must unfailingly forgive others before we have any hope of the forgiveness of God ourselves. Such a reading would fly in the face of a gospel of unearned grace, in which the king takes the initiative, removing the burden of an enormous debt that can never be repaid.

If we are to learn anything from Jesus' warnings, however, it's that God lovingly sacrificed his only Son that we might be forgiven, and thus expects his people to demonstrate the same mercy-filled character. Our refusal to forgive others may indicate that we have neither fully nor humbly understood what we ourselves have already been forgiven, or what we still need to be forgiven each day.

Put simply, God takes forgiveness seriously, and so must we.

But before we discuss forgiveness more fully, let's address the other side. As mentioned at the beginning of the chapter, sometimes we are the one offended—but other times we are the offender. Are we willing to admit it? If we value peace, we need to learn how to apologize with both humility and compassion.

The Many Ways of Saying "Sorry"

God has made peace between us and him, and calls us to make peace with each other. Sin, however, disrupts peace in both of these arenas of relationship. And when we sin against God—not if, but when!—we are directed to seek God's forgiveness through confession (1 John 1:8-10).

The word translated as "confess" suggests a heartfelt agreement with God about our sin.[5] When, with regret, we admit what we've done, God faithfully restores the relationship, and sets us back on the right path.

When we sin against each other, both apology and forgiveness are needed.

But this isn't just a matter of our private relationship with God. We are also counseled in Scripture to confess our sins to each other (e.g., James 5:16).[6] In short, when we sin against each other, including in marriage, both apology and forgiveness are needed to repair the relationship.

In the final section of this chapter, I will describe a process for pursuing peace that applies to both apology and forgiveness. It's no accident that similar virtues are needed from both directions: the humility to admit your own brokenness, whether to yourself or to your spouse; the compassion to empathize with your spouse's brokenness; the desire and the commitment to make things right between you. The need for apology and forgiveness may flare up around specific incidents, but these events are often interpreted against the background of a whole history of relationship in which each spouse has felt victimized in turn. What often stymies apology, in other words, even when we clearly know we're in the wrong, is some unacknowledged resentment of our own—not necessarily toward our spouse—that makes apologizing feel unfair.

To confess and to forgive, therefore, are like two sides of a coin, and will be addressed together in the process that will be described at the end of the chapter. For the remainder of this section, we'll explore a practical reason why even some well-meant apologies still fail: the recipient believes something important is missing.

As Gary Chapman and Jennifer Thomas have argued, people have convictions and expectations about what constitutes a "real" or valid apology.[7] The problem is that couples often differ on these "apology languages," without necessarily realizing it.[8] One spouse's language isn't better or more "right" than the other's—but if they can't connect on that score, attempts at reconciliation may actually drive them further apart. Chapman and Thomas describe five such apology languages: (1) expressing regret, (2) accepting responsibility, (3) making restitution, (4) genuinely repenting, and (5) requesting forgiveness.

To identify your own preference, begin asking yourself three questions. First, if your spouse were to truly apologize to you, what would you expect him or her to say or do? Second, and conversely, if you remember a time when your spouse's apology felt inappropriate or insincere, what was missing? And finally, if you were to apologize to someone else, and do it well, what would *you* do?[9] All of these answers will point toward your taken-for-granted assumptions about "good" apologies. Then read the explanations below, and see if they help you make sense of what has or hasn't worked in your marriage.

Regret. The first and perhaps most obvious language of apology is to let your spouse know that you truly regret what you have done. In some cases, simply saying "I'm sorry" may suffice—but only if he or she can tell that you really mean it.

Many of us as children were forced to apologize to our siblings and playmates when we didn't want to, or when we didn't feel we had done anything wrong. Our parents demanded that we say, "I'm sorry," whether we meant it or not. The unfortunate result is that we may come to adulthood feeling that merely mouthing the words should absolve us of blame: "I'm sorry" is supposed to get us out of trouble, even if we haven't a clue why our spouse is upset. We may even resent it when his or her forgiveness isn't automatic, huffing, "Well, I said I was sorry! What more do you want?"

The "more," of course, is humility and empathy. Your words and body language should clearly communicate that you understand what you've done and how your spouse feels about it. You may be tempted to defend yourself, saying, "I'm sorry if I hurt you, *but…*" Don't do it. That's a non-apology that will send the wrong message: "I don't understand why you're hurt, and you shouldn't feel that way." Not much empathy there.

Bottom line, your spouse may need some tangible sign that you truly regret the pain you've caused, and honestly saying "sorry" can help.

Responsibility. How many moments in movie and television comedy poke fun at our inability to choke out the words, "I was wrong"? Taking personal responsibility for our actions and their consequences requires humility. Some of us are loath to admit any error; it may feel like our self-worth is at stake, or that we're being falsely accused, at least in part.

You don't have to agree completely with everything your spouse may be saying. But you do need to admit to whatever peace-violating part you've played—without excuses. For example, in the midst of an argument, did you lose your temper and respond in a demeaning or hurtful way? Even if your anger was justified, you can still humbly own up to what you know you did wrong: "I lost control and said some really mean things. There's no excuse for that."

And again: don't contaminate the confession by tacking on a "but." That sends the message that you're really not to blame, which invalidates the whole apology.

Restitution. Our spouses may appreciate the "I'm sorry" and the confession of guilt. But to them, talk is cheap. In order to believe that the apology is sincere, they need to see some attempt at restitution. In some cases, there may be actual reparations to make: something that's been damaged needs to be fixed.

More broadly, what our offended spouses may need is some concrete sign of care and concern. Here, Chapman and Thomas build on Chapman's earlier notion of the five "love languages," suggesting that we need to know what kind of behavior uniquely communicates love to our spouses.[10]

If, for example, your spouse's primary love language is *words of affirmation*, it would help if your apology included a sincere statement of what you love and appreciate about him or her. If it's *acts of service*, back up your apology by doing something helpful to ease your spouse's load. If your spouse feels loved through *receiving gifts*, come up with something you know he or she would appreciate. How much you spend isn't the issue—the thoughtfulness behind the gift is.

Perhaps your spouse's primary love language is *quality time*. If so, your apology can't be rushed; you need to set aside a specific and undistracted time when you can focus on being completely attentive. And finally, if your spouse craves *physical touch*, your apology may feel incomplete unless you hold his or her hand or give a warm hug.

Repentance. In some couples, the words "I'm sorry" or even attempts at restitution may come easily. But then the same offense keeps happening, and soon even the most passionate apology falls on deaf ears. As one wife said, "He apologizes. He promises not to do it again. Then he does it again… I don't want 'sorry.' I want him not to do the thing that bothers me—ever!"[11]

When you apologize to your spouse, you may be sincere about change—at that moment. But don't expect credit or appreciation for your good intentions if change doesn't happen. Broken promises only add to the hurt and resentment.

If repentance is your spouse's apology language, Chapman and Thomas make three practical recommendations that will help you follow through. First, clearly *verbalize* to your spouse both your intention and your desire to mend your ways. Don't keep it to yourself; make a commitment and be accountable.

Second, *make a plan.* Be specific about what changes are needed, in terms of what you will do and when. If you're not sure what would be appropriate, ask your spouse for help; it can be a good exercise for your spouse to clearly articulate what he or she really needs to see in terms of change.

Finally, once you have a workable plan, *write it down*: this step not only provides a concrete reminder, but helps avoid future disagreements about what was promised.[12]

Requesting. If it's difficult for some of us to tell our spouse, "I'm sorry," it may be doubly difficult to say, "Will you please forgive me?" The latter makes us more vulnerable by leaving the outcome in his or her hands. What if the answer is "No," or "I'm not sure," or "I'm not ready yet"? How long are we willing to stay in the humbling position of the penitent?

For some spouses, however, that's precisely the point. Asking for forgiveness may feel like we're giving up too much control, opening ourselves to being shamed for our weakness or failure. That's risky. But if we *don't* ask, our apology may seem manipulative or insincere.

The words we use to request forgiveness can be simple: some variation on "please forgive me" will often do. But it's the attitude that counts. Requesting is not insisting, or cajoling, or demanding. We are quite literally putting ourselves at the mercy of our spouses, leaving them to decide whether they will forgive us or not.

And then we must wait: wait on our spouses, and even more importantly, wait on God.

ꕥ

Whatever you do in good conscience to apologize to your spouse, he or she may still be looking for particular words or actions that signal that you really mean it. That's neither stubbornness nor arrogance—though it may feel like that if your apology is rejected! If you really want to make a connection, if reconciliation is truly your goal, have empathy for your spouse's pain and what he or she needs to see or hear from you to begin the healing process.

What if you're the one who's been offended, and your spouse isn't getting the apology "right"? Armed with the knowledge of possible differences in your apology languages, prayerfully muster the humility and compassion necessary to see if there's *any* reason to believe that he or she is being sincere. If so, don't leave your spouse groping and guessing. Don't assume that your spouse already knows what you want or need. Tell him. Tell her.

All of this is in the service of helping a well-intentioned apology find its mark. And often, forgiveness follows quickly. But not always. Is the offended spouse obliged to forgive? What should a peacemaker do?

What We've Been Given, What We Must Give

If apology is complicated, forgiveness can be more so, for a number of related reasons. We may pass over the need for forgiveness too lightly, waving off apologies with a half-hearted, "Forget it, it's no big deal"—when in fact it still feels bigger than we're willing to admit. Or we resist forgiveness—and especially reconciliation—because it feels risky and unwise. We feel victimized, and need our anger as a shield to protect us from being hurt again. Our friends may even tell us that we'd be saps to forgive.

Forgiveness may feel unfair or unjust. Aren't our spouses guilty of doing something wrong? Don't they deserve to be punished? It just doesn't seem right to let them off the hook, at least not easily. And we may refuse to forgive because we're not done having our revenge. That's not to say that we're plotting a capital crime, but if the truth be told, we get some satisfaction from their suffering, even it's only their anxious uncertainty about whether we'll ever let go of the grudge.

As said earlier, Jesus has called us—*commanded* us—to be merciful, forgiving people. But if we're honest, we have to confess that there are times that we just don't *want* to forgive, for any or all of the reasons above. The commandment grates on our moral nerves and offends our sense of fair play and entitlement.

Psychologist Everett Worthington, for example, has conducted some of the most creative and instructive research on forgiveness. But his interest isn't merely academic. One of his books about forgiveness opens with the story of his mother's murder: when she surprised a burglar in her home (or possibly two), he bludgeoned her with a crowbar, vandalized the house, and fled. A devout Christian, Worthington writes with soul-searching honesty about the sleepless night he endured after hearing the grisly details. Pacing the bedroom, he wrestled with a furious desire for revenge:

> I stormed about, rehearsing scenes of violence and anger... I was eyeball to eyeball with my convictions—carefully thought out in times unclouded by emotion. But the impact of this death and the horror of my images of what my mother must have experienced were an in-your-face confrontation. They rocked my sense of identity. I thought I knew my own character. ...I wanted my hands on that murderer. I did not even want to consider mercy.[13]

What can one do in such a situation? What's the way forward? We can try to obey for the sake of religious obedience alone, forgiving as best we can, albeit with gritted teeth. In all likelihood, that will lead neither to true forgiveness nor reconciliation, but to emotional and spiritual exhaustion, as we struggle to let go not only of our resentment toward the other, but possibly toward a God who simply asks too much of his followers.[14]

Or we can take a more therapeutic route. As Anne Lamott has observed wryly, "not forgiving is like drinking rat poison and then waiting for the rat to die."[15] Bitterness poisons our soul, we're told; thus, we are encouraged to forgive because it's good for *us.* If we let go of our gnawing resentment, we may find emotional freedom.[16]

In some ways, that's sound advice. There is plenty of evidence documenting the impact of negative emotions on our health, and continuing to ruminate on the past can send these emotions into an ever-worsening spiral of anxiety, sadness, and anger.[17] Conversely, releasing our resentment through forgiveness has positive benefits. As psychiatrist Edward Hallowell has written:

> When you forgive, you free yourself from mind-forged manacles. …Among the many health benefits, your blood pressure may go down, your resting heart rate may decrease, your immune system may get stronger, your susceptibility to a heart attack or a stroke may decrease, headaches and backaches and neck pain may abate… Forgiving lifts your spirits. It makes you feel happier, and it clarifies your thinking. No longer must you carry a lodestone of anger and resentment.[18]

Hallowell tells the story of Marietta Jaeger, whose seven-year-old daughter Susie was kidnapped. What parent wouldn't nurse feelings of hatred and vengeance in such a situation? But Jaeger wrestled inside, caught between the anger she knew was justified and her Christian principles. She made a deliberate decision to obey her conscience and forgive the kidnapper.

Not that forgiveness came immediately or easily. She had to make the same obedient decision over and over as a daily discipline:

> I've heard people say that forgiveness is for wimps. Well, I say then that they must never have tried it. Forgiveness is hard work. It demands diligent self-discipline, constant corralling of our basest instincts, custody of the tongue, and a steadfast refusal not to get caught up in the mean-spiritedness of our times. It doesn't mean we forget, we condone, or we absolve responsibility. It does mean that we let go of hate, that we try to separate the loss and the cost from the recompense or punishment we deem is due.[19]

After a year, she still had no news of Susie's whereabouts. Interviewed about her experience for a newspaper article, Jaeger expressed concern for both her daughter and the kidnapper, and even the desire to talk to him directly.

The night the article came out, the kidnapper called. The man on the telephone taunted her mercilessly about how powerless she was: *he* was in control, and there was nothing she could do about it. But Jaeger had already been pursuing forgiveness for a year, and in that moment, she reached deeply into her values and surprised even herself with her ability to let go of her rage and desire to strike back.

She wasn't the only one who was surprised.

They talked for more than an hour. At one point, when she reached out in compassion to ask how she could be of service to him, he broke down and wept, feeling the crushing weight of his guilt. The man had not only kidnapped Susie, but had murdered her. He deserved death. But even then, Jaeger didn't want revenge to sully the memory of her beautiful child. She therefore testified on the murderer's behalf, pleading for leniency, and the man received life imprisonment instead of the death penalty. Jaeger speaks eloquently of her reasons for forgiving even such a heinous crime:

> Though I readily admit that initially I wanted to kill this man with my bare hands…I was convinced that my best and healthiest option was to forgive. … However justified, our unforgiveness undoes us. Anger, hatred, resentment, bitterness, revenge—they are death-dealing spirits, and they will "take our lives" on some level as surely as Susie's life was taken. I believe the only way we can be whole, healthy, happy persons is to learn to forgive. … Though I would never have chosen it so, the first person to receive a gift from the death of my daughter…was me.[20]

The emphasis here is on what's best for us: forgiveness is a personally healthier path than revenge. Even when it is justified, bitterness comes at a high emotional and spiritual price.

But it's also important to realize that even in her own telling of the story, as in the story of Immaculée Ilibagiza, the full fruition of forgiveness came not in the gift of freedom she received, but in the gift of mercy she was finally able to offer to the man who had murdered a loved one. When we've been the victims of injustice, when our emotions are still raw, embracing forgiveness as a gift we give *ourselves* may be the easier door to enter. The biblical understanding, however, the one more consistent with the mercy God extends to us, is that forgiveness is a gift we give to *others*.

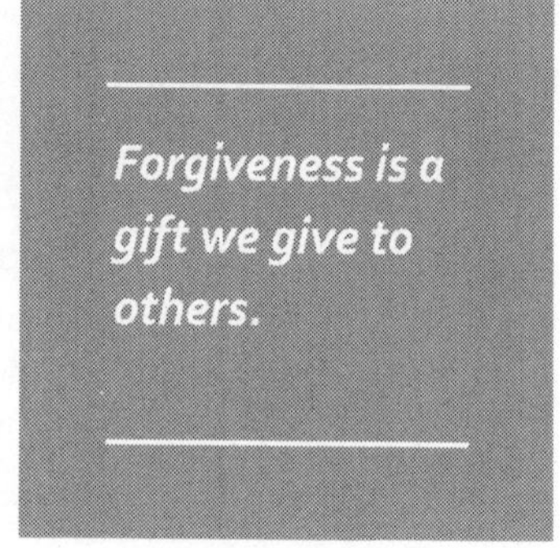
Forgiveness is a gift we give to others.

Worthington has succinctly and memorably put it this way: "We've all heard 'Forgive and forget,' but forgiving seems to be for *giving*, not for *getting*."[21] The statement is based on his own research, in which he compared the results of programs that taught participants to forgive. One kind of program promoted forgiveness as a benefit to oneself; the other encouraged people to forgive altruistically, empathizing with the offender's fallible and fragile humanity.

Not surprisingly, the people in the second group took longer to convince. But the results were clear. As Worthington summarizes, "forgiving in order to bless the person who hurt him or her [produced] more and longer-lasting forgiveness than forgiving just for the person's own benefit."[22]

Think back to Jesus' story of the merciful king and his unmerciful servant. The servant had racked up an enormous debt, and the king had every right to repayment. But seeing the servant's impossible plight, the king was moved to compassion and released the man from every last penny of debt. No self-serving motive was involved, only mercy—and the king rightly expected the forgiven servant to be merciful in turn to his own debtors.

Biblical forgiveness, the kind that best embodies the cause of God's shalom, is pure gift, an act of undeserved mercy. If it feels unfair to forgive the wrongs we've suffered from others, well, that's because in some ways it is. When we forgive, we are making an intentional decision to extend God's grace as a gift to others instead of insisting on payback and retribution.

Why would we do such a thing? Because we know deep, deep down that this is how God deals with us and our sin.

Let it be said and said clearly: to forgive as God forgives does not mean to condone wrongdoing. God's ongoing work is to restore peace to what sin has spoiled; forgiveness, therefore, can't mean ignoring sin like doting but irresponsible parents who conveniently look the other way when their kids misbehave.

Rather, godly forgiveness openly acknowledges the sin *in order to* condemn it. That's why some people refuse to accept the words, "I forgive you"—because the statement implies a guilt to which the other may not be ready to confess. But in forgiveness, condemnation isn't the final word. Mercy is. The one who forgives releases the offender from the burden of guilt and the claim of justice.

In a world in which sin still holds sway, there will always be people who treat others with jaw-dropping rudeness or even malice. There will be still be moments in our marriages in which we are inconsiderate, dismissive, or even contemptuous toward one another. And there will always be a part of us that nurtures self-righteous indignation and thoughts of revenge.

True, underneath the revenge, there may be a valid desire for justice in the form of retribution. Nobody wants to live in a world in which there is no moral accountability and the guilty go their merry way unpunished. Nor should we.

But consider the kind of world that a resentful desire for retribution would create, in which everyone insisted on what they believed was fairly due. Every misdemeanor and misstep, no matter how slight, would have to be handled with exacting, eye-for-eye justice. In our marriages, every thoughtless word and careless deed would be meticulously recorded, and every hurt feeling painstakingly repaid. Would that bring peace to our relationships? Not likely. Martin Luther King was right: "The old law of an eye for an eye leaves everybody blind."[23]

What's the alternative? Forgiveness. God, in holiness, cannot condone sin. But love is just as important an expression of divine holiness as justice, and it is forgiveness that brings the two together. As Miroslav Volf has written:

> The world is sinful. That's why God doesn't affirm it indiscriminately. God loves the world. That's why God doesn't punish it in justice. What does God do with this double bind? God forgives.[24]

And as peacemakers, we are called to be people of mercy ourselves, people who embody both love and justice, who demonstrate God's forgiving character in their relationships. Without a vision of peace, forgiveness may seem like a sucker's bet. All of the virtues discussed in this book will be needed to help us become imperfect but willing conduits of God's mercy, even in our homes.

I know: it's easier said than done. Letting go of our resentment and anger can be a long and difficult process. God in his grace may quickly and miraculously take away all of our hurt and vengeful feelings. But that's not typical, especially in the case of greater or repeated offenses; full forgiveness comes with time and discipline, if indeed it comes at all. Most days, we will probably still need to confess that we simply don't *want* to love our enemies—we're not done being offended yet!—and ask again and again for God's help.

In short, forgiveness must begin with a humble and grateful acceptance of the mercy we've already received from God, and that gratitude is meant to extend outward in mercy toward others. Forgiveness is for giving, a generous gift that peacemakers endeavor to share with others.

How do we begin the journey toward forgiveness? Again, the issues are complex. It's possible to be in such denial of one's hurt and anger that we forgive too quickly and superficially. Or we may make a magnanimous show of doling out forgiveness to people who didn't ask for it and don't want it. Or we may say we forgive our spouses, then continue to punish them in some way while feigning innocence. Because of these and other complications, whole volumes have been written on the subject. Some of them are cited in the notes at the end of this book.

The practical process described in the next section assumes either that you are consciously upset about something your spouse has said or done, and are willing to consider the possibility of forgiveness, or that you are the one who is considering making an apology. The process is built on all the interlocking virtues discussed earlier: a humility that admits weakness and grieves sin; a spiritual hunger and hope that compel us to pursue peace; a compassion that humanizes rather than a resentment that demonizes. While the emphasis will be on forgiving, the steps described also explore the application of these same virtues to apologizing.

First, however, a word of caution. In this chapter, I have told stories of Christians who were able to follow the merciful example of Jesus even in the most extreme situations. No one would have begrudged these people the right to their anger and resentment. But each came to the conclusion that forgiveness was necessary. Through their own dogged persistence and the grace of God, they found their hearts transformed, and thereby experienced peace.

Against the background of such horrific tales, the offenses we suffer in our marriages may seem minor by comparison. But we must remember a crucial difference between their situation and ours: they didn't have to live with the people they forgave.

Every marriage carries within it the seeds of manipulation and violence: verbal, emotional, physical. Regardless of how adorable and innocent everyone may look in the wedding pictures, every wife has a sinful husband, and every husband has a sinful wife.

Moreover, we bring the brokenness experienced in our previous relationships—including the families we grew up in—to the marriage union itself. The injuries we suffer today, great and small, echo old injustices and reactivate familiar doubts and fears. When that happens, home may no longer feel like a safe and welcoming place.

The process of forgiveness offers a path to reconciliation. But prayerful wisdom is needed. In a deeply broken world such as ours, it cannot be assumed that every relationship *should* be reconciled. A victim of domestic violence, for example, may learn to forgive from the heart—but that doesn't entail a requirement to endure continued abuse. As said earlier, forgiveness doesn't ignore or condone sin, nor is it incompatible with a justly given demand for change.

Again, remember Jesus' parable of the unforgiving servant. The king had every right to have the debt repaid, but instead compassionately released the servant from the entire burden. The morally clueless debtor, unfortunately, lost no time showing just how unworthy he was of such clemency. The king didn't turn a blind eye. If the servant refused to live by mercy, he would have to live with retribution.

Forgiveness doesn't condone sin, nor is it incompatible with a justly given demand for change.

The point, of course, is not that we get to take revenge if our spouse doesn't apologize or change. That is clearly not the way of peace, and vengeance belongs to God alone (Romans 12:18-19). But we must also recognize that not every act of mercy—even from God!—begets repentance. Not everything done for the sake of peace brings the desired result.

We can hope that forgiveness opens the door to reconciliation and healing in marriage. Many times it will. But sometimes it won't. We may need to content ourselves with hope itself, with the larger vision of God's shalom and the work to which we are committed as peacemakers.

Steps Along the Way

Below I will suggest several "steps" along the path to apology and forgiveness. They are neither a foolproof formula nor an unbreakable sequence; one seldom goes straight from point A to point B in the spiritual life. Depending on your situation, some steps will be more like way stations, places to stop for a while to pray, meditate, and even argue with God before continuing. And you may need to circle back to some of these stations again and again. Don't rush the process. Take the time needed to let the Holy Spirit transform you from the inside out.

Is God already prompting you toward apologizing to or forgiving your spouse for something? Begin by identifying and thinking about the area or incident in question. And remember: this isn't about trying to appease a God who has grown impatient and irritated with you. As the psalmist says, "The Lord is close to the brokenhearted" (Psalm 34:18). God is patient and kind, and wants you to know his peace. You can be honest with him about your thoughts and feelings, even the ones that may seem unacceptable. With that in mind, therefore, use the steps as focal points for prayer, meditation, and reflection.

Accept the fact that we live in a sin-ridden world. If you haven't hardened yourself to it, you see the reality of sin all the time, everywhere. People hurt other people; they act selfishly, maliciously, or stupidly. "Accepting" the fact of sin means neither helpless resignation nor approval. But it also means more than just an impersonal acknowledgement of sin at an intellectual level.

As Jesus said in the Beatitudes, "Happy are people who grieve" (Matt 5:4), who regret the ways in which the world is out of kilter with God's good intent for creation. To forgive truly, you need to see the world as it truly is, and not just as you would wish it to be. There is beauty, to be sure, and much to inspire both gratitude and wonder; but there is also ugliness and much to mourn. Some of the ugliness is ours to confess; some is for us to forgive, knowing that to do so is not to minimize evil, but to face it with faith and courage.

Accept the fact that there is sin and brokenness in your own marriage. The sin we grieve is not just "out there" but "in here": in our relationships, our homes, our marriages. As one writer has put it, "All marriages are mended garments"—less like designer couture, perhaps, than workaday clothing with awkwardly sewn patches.[25]

As described in the previous chapter, we all bring hopes and dreams to marriage, even if we're not aware of them until an expectation is violated or a dream is dashed. Even if you've never thought of your spouse as your "soul mate," you may have harbored other hopes: *This is the person who will finally and fully love and accept me for who I am. This is the person whom I can trust in every way. This is the one who will help me grow closer to God. This is the one who will balance my weaknesses and help me be strong.*

At some level, in other words, apology and forgiveness are about disappointed expectations. You may discover, for example, that in some fashion, by temperament or personality, your spouse seems almost constitutionally incapable of meeting your ideal of a husband or wife. You may be disappointed in yourself. And you must come to terms with the fact that both you and your spouse are fallible human beings, flawed in ways you may not have anticipated before marriage, ways that sometimes matter deeply to you.

Accepting the reality of brokenness in your marriage, therefore, is more than just flippantly agreeing that "Nobody's perfect." When it comes to deeper hurts, it may mean grieving the loss of a dream.

If you're not aware of any disappointed hopes or expectations, try this. Imagine that before you go to bed tonight, you pray that God would do a miracle in your marriage. If you're the one who's been offended, your prayer would be for God to change your spouse in the way that matters most to you right now; if you're the one considering an apology, your prayer would be for God to change *you*. What would you need to see in your spouse or yourself to know that God had indeed done the miracle?[26] What would be different? How would you feel about the change? Why is it important to you? Questions like these can help you figure out what you're really wishing for your marriage, and thus where your ambivalence about forgiving or apologizing may be stuck.

With compassion for yourself, recognize the ways in which you bring your own vulnerability and brokenness to the marriage. Think back to what I said in the previous chapter about the personal vulnerabilities we bring with us into marriage: the needs we have for feelings of security, freedom, admiration, approval, control. Other needs could be named. But the point is that we tend to see our spouse's behavior through the lenses of our need, making us more reactive to some offenses than others.

Tactless comments from a spouse might sting, for example, but they hurt more deeply when we crave admiration and approval. We may be legitimately upset if a spouse spontaneously spends more money out of a joint account than we think wise; but at least part of our resentment of their "recklessness" may be driven by our own needs for security and control. And if we're the ones being accused of doing wrong, it may be harder to admit failure in areas that are tied to our sense of self-worth or competence.

Have you been hurt by your spouse's behavior? Unless you've misunderstood the situation (never discount the possibility!), part of your anger is probably righteous indignation. You *should* be offended by injustice, large or small, including the injustice that happens in your own home. But beneath your irritation or exasperation may lie a deeper sense of loss or fear that needs to be acknowledged and understood. This is where you feel the offense most keenly, and it's from there that the strongest resistance to forgiving will spring.

Why is it so hard sometimes to forgive, to let go of anger and resentment? To some extent, it's because we need our anger; it acts like a shield, holding the offender at bay, trying to protect us against further insult. But it can also wall us off from our own more threatening emotions, where the injury is most deeply felt. That's why some marital arguments go on endlessly: we're fighting about the wrong thing. We quarrel over a particular behavior, but never get to the underlying pain the behavior has triggered. Anger feels safer; "I'm mad" is more manageable than "My wife betrayed me," or "I can't count on my husband," or even, "Nobody cares."

So ask yourself: is there some grief or fear hiding self-protectively behind your anger? Can you identify it? With compassion for yourself, embrace the fact that this is part of the brokenness you bring to your marriage. To forgive fully means granting mercy from that humble place of vulnerability. And for many, this could be a good place to seek counsel from a therapist or a wise and trustworthy pastor or friend, someone who could provide a safe environment for self-exploration.

A similar humility, of course, is needed if you're the one feeling responsible for the hurt. You have your own vulnerabilities; it may feel threatening to admit, even to yourself, that you've done something wrong or made a mistake. Maybe it even feels a little unfair; a voice inside you is complaining, "Why is it always *my* fault?" But that may be your vulnerabilities talking, trying to keep you from taking a humble position that feels risky and powerless.

Such is the tragedy of how brokenness and sin disrupt a marriage. Both of you may feel injured in your own way. Both of you need comfort from the other. But both of you may also be too preoccupied with putting up shields to give or receive it.

Somebody has to break the impasse. If you know that you've given offense in any way, the initiative is yours to take. Start by admitting to yourself the vulnerabilities that make it difficult to say you're sorry. Compassionately accept that this is part of who you are; it will be harder to apologize non-defensively if you don't.

Meditate on the gift of grace you have already received from God, and the grace you still need each day. Biblically speaking, knowing what we've been forgiven is the fount of our ability to forgive others. We've seen this already in the teaching of Jesus, and we find it also in Paul: "Put aside all bitterness, losing your temper, anger, shouting, and slander, along with every other evil. Be kind, compassionate, and forgiving to each other, in the same way God forgave you in Christ" (Ephesians 4:31-32). Cultivating gratitude for God's mercy, therefore, can help you be more merciful; meditating on his grace can help soften and transform your feelings of bitterness and rage, paving the way for compassion and forgiveness.

It can also pave the way for a more sincere apology. Let's face it: it's hard to listen to blame or admit fault when we crave acceptance and avoid rejection. But a gospel that brings together divine love and justice declares a liberating truth: we are both deeply blameworthy, and deeply loved. By the sheer mercy of God, we are simultaneously cracked pots and vessels of glory.

God is faithful, just, and forgiving (1 John 1:9); his nature is love, and he wants to see his love perfected in our relationships to one another (1 John 4:11-21). Once we begin to truly grasp who God is, we can confess our sins to him more freely, without fear of rejection.

Admittedly, confessing to your spouse is a riskier proposition. He or she may not be ready to forgive. But your contribution to peace begins with confessing humbly and honestly to God, confident of his grace.

Consider carefully what your identity as a Christian demands in this situation. Some readers, I imagine, might wonder why I didn't put this step earlier in the list. If we call ourselves Christians, and Jesus commands that we forgive, shouldn't we just obey and be done with it? Why all this stuff about expectations and feelings?

Some people may be able to forgive fully and freely, all in a moment, solely as a matter of Christian duty. But I would suspect that, apart from a miraculous intervention of the Spirit, this only happens after years of faithful discipleship, or what Eugene Peterson once called "a long obedience in the same direction."[27]

On the one hand, our emotions are part of who we are, both as cracked pots and as those created in God's image. Denying them doesn't make them go away, and they will inevitably come into play whenever we seek to apologize or forgive. On the other hand, in the midst of our ambivalence, we may also need to remind ourselves that obedience sometimes means doing the right thing even if our emotions aren't fully aligned.

You are a Christian, which means you have committed yourself to *follow* Christ. What might that commitment mean, concretely, in the situation at hand?

Ask yourself whether you really desire God's peace. The whole premise of this book is that God desires to restore his shalom to a good creation that has been damaged by sin. Those who follow Christ are called to be peacemakers, which includes being conscious channels of God's peace in our marriages. Empowered by the Spirit, we can treat every offense and every misstep as an opportunity to pursue peace rather than retribution.

This is a matter of vision and imagination. It's one thing to apologize or forgive begrudgingly because we think we have to, like kids forced to make up after a fight. It's another to actually hunger for things to be put right, with an attitude of hope in the faithfulness of God.

Hallowell advises those seeking to forgive to ask themselves, "What do I want my pain to turn into?"[28] It's an excellent question to ponder on either side, whether you're asking mercy or granting it. Can you imagine God working through your situation to establish peace? Go back to chapter 2, if needed; immerse yourself in a vision of shalom, and try to reimagine your pain in light of that vision.

Make a decision as to what path you will pursue. At some point, of course, you will need to decide what to do and commit to it. If you're going to apologize or forgive, make the decision concrete. Write it in your journal. Tell God. Tell a trustworthy friend: one who's a good listener and not given to gossip.

My choice of wording above, however, is deliberate: you are not just choosing the *behavior* of apologizing or forgiving, but the *path* that the behavior represents, the long and winding path of peace. A humble apology, for example, might take only minutes, but you might have to remain in that humble posture as you wait weeks or even months to be forgiven.

That's because forgiveness itself is often an ongoing process. Today, you may say, "I forgive you," and mean it. But tomorrow, the old pain and desire for vengeance may spring up again, and you'll have to commit yourself anew to the path you've chosen, circling back if necessary to some of the steps described earlier.

Be encouraged. The fullness of God's shalom is our future and final destination, but we can still experience moments of peace in the meantime. God, in other words, doesn't just stand at the end of the road with his arms crossed, waiting for you to hurry up and get there. He is with you every step of the way.

Have compassion for your spouse. Earlier, I asked you to come to terms with the fact of brokenness in your marriage, and to have compassion for your own vulnerability. If you've decided to pursue the path of peace, it's time to broaden that compassion to include your spouse.

Why apologize? Because your spouse has been hurt, presumably by something you've said or done. Hopefully, if you can see past your defensiveness, it will be relatively easy to empathize; the reason for his or her pain may seem obvious, because you would feel the same way if the tables were turned. But it's also possible that your spouse's pain will make little sense to you at all; that's not how *you* would have reacted, and it's hard to escape the feeling that he or she is being silly or unreasonable, making mountains out of molehills.

The latter scenario is all too common; yet empathy, while more difficult, is still much needed. Starting with compassion for your own woundedness will help you set down your self-protective shield for a moment. But then you must reach out in compassion to your wounded spouse. Allow yourself to be moved by his or her pain. If you can, use your imagination and what you already know about your spouse's background to try to understand from the inside out how he or she experienced the offense.

"Well, of course!" one might respond. "Isn't it obvious that the offender should have compassion for the suffering he or she has caused?" In a more ideal world, perhaps. But that's not the way it usually works. As the accused, we may minimize or rationalize away our behavior, sometimes even blaming the victim. If and when we offer an apology, we may do so to quickly end an uncomfortable argument, bypassing the inconvenient distress of compassion. And from the other side, we who have been hurt sometimes accept apologies a bit half-heartedly; what we really want is compassion and understanding, but we settle for a quick apology because we figure it's all we're going to get.

True peacemakers must do better. And strikingly, according to the teaching and example of Jesus himself, that includes not just the compassion offenders should have for those whom they have hurt, but the reverse: the gift of compassionate mercy forgivers are to extend to their offenders.

It's easy, for example, to demonize those who have harmed us, reacting as if they had targeted us deliberately. And sadly, sometimes that's true. But typically, marital squabbles are less like war and more like bad choreography: two partners dancing different dances, stepping on each other's toes, and thinking the other is to blame.

Blame demonizes, but compassion humanizes. That's not to say that the blame isn't deserved. But our way of going about it often reduces others to one-dimensional stock characters in a private morality play; we imagine them as villains, so we can be the hero.

Blame demonizes; compassion humanizes.

Real life, of course, is far more complicated. "Villains," it turns out, have more complex motivations than we may wish to admit. They have their own way of seeing and experiencing the world, and just like us—surprise!—they have their own vulnerabilities.

So if you're the one who's been offended, try this: instead of resenting your spouse for the role he or she has played in your story, try to reimagine your spouse as the main character in his or her own story, a story that may include past hurts and present challenges, emotional vulnerabilities and disappointed dreams. Against that background, how might your spouse have experienced the situation differently than you did? How might that difference help you make some sense of what he or she did that hurt you? I'm not asking you to condone the behavior, but to understand it as best you can, the better to develop a little empathy for your spouse's humanity.

Give your spouse the gift of mercy. Once more, think back to the parables of Jesus. A despised Samaritan put himself at risk to care for a fellow traveler who lay wounded by the side of the road. A king took pity on a hapless servant, releasing him from a debt that he had every right to collect. Both were acts of mercy; both were given as examples for us to follow.

Are you ready to make your compassion concrete? If you're going to apologize to a wounded spouse, be careful not to do it haphazardly. Make a plan: choose a good time and place, free of distractions; consider your spouse's apology language; write out the words you'll use, read them over carefully, then rewrite them as many times as needed. Edit out anything that hints of "It's not really my fault," or "Actually, you're partially to blame." These ways of apologizing are like giving a gift and then immediately taking it back—which can be worse than not giving a gift at all.

Indeed, the image of a gift is particularly appropriate in the case of forgiveness. As psychologist Robert Enright has written:

> Forgiving is an act of mercy toward an offender, someone who does not necessarily deserve our mercy. It is a gift to our offender for the purpose of changing the relationship between ourselves and those who have hurt us.[29]

Whether you verbally say, "I forgive you," or write it out in a letter (the latter will be easier for many), you are releasing your spouse from the prison of your resentment.

But note the phrase, "changing the relationship." In a more immediate sense, it can mean overcoming the enmity created by the offense. The emotional temperature of a home can become quite chilly when one spouse offends another, and forgiveness often helps restore warmth.

At another level, however, the phrase reminds us that forgiveness carries an implicit expectation: the offense should not happen again. The king in Jesus' parable does not forgive the debt in order for the servant to say, "Whew! I dodged that bullet," and go right back to his financially irresponsible ways. He is expected to change.

If you're the one doing the forgiving, therefore, don't just say, "Forget about it." Your spouse *should* remember the offense itself, the pain it caused, and your words of mercy—at least well enough to want to avoid going down that road again.

And to be realistic, more hurtful offenses aren't likely to vanish from your memory either. To forgive includes a two-sided commitment: internally, you stop yourself from nursing the grievance or ruminating over the offense; externally, you refrain from bringing it up in conversation to needle your spouse.

But even then, don't be surprised if the pain resurfaces occasionally. After all, we're wired to remember pain; it helps us to avoid putting ourselves in harm's way. Without the protective function of pain, we probably wouldn't even survive childhood!

Plan, therefore, to revisit the process of cultivating compassion for both yourself and your spouse as often as needed. It may take continued commitment for your feelings to finally and fully catch up with the merciful decision you've made.

Mercy is a gift, and the giver cannot control how the gift will be received. As said earlier, forgiveness doesn't always result in a corresponding repentance. You can give your spouse the benefit of the doubt; real change, after all, may take time. But don't confuse forgiveness with a free pass for your spouse to do as he or she pleases; again, to quote Enright: "Forgiveness is free; trust must be earned."[30]

❧☙

Apology and forgiveness, repentance and mercy: in real-life marriages, this can be tricky territory. It can't be reduced to a technique or a procedure. At their best, both apology and forgiveness are tangible expressions of all the virtues cherished by those who desire peace. Abundant humility and compassion are needed on both sides. These qualities must be cultivated even when the marriage is going well, or else they will be much harder to draw upon when things are going poorly. The truth is that even as Christians, husbands and wives hurt and wound each other, sometimes willfully, sometimes not. The question is not whether such things will happen, but whether we will respond as peacemakers when they do.

❧☙

Questions for discussion and reflection:

Note: *Discussing the topics of apology and forgiveness may provoke strong emotions and the memory of deep hurts. It is essential to maintain a safe and caring environment. Here are some beginning guidelines:*

- *Everyone in the conversation must be committed to listening with care and compassion. Refrain from giving advice unless it is specifically and directly requested.*
- *Don't tell others outside the group about what you've heard—not even in the form of a prayer request!—unless there are clear legal reasons to do so, or you have the person's permission.*
- *Take breaks as needed to give people an opportunity to calm down.*
- *Group leaders: if possible, have referral information at hand for those group members who may wish to consult with trustworthy counselors. If you are referring a couple for counseling, be sure the counselor has training and experience in working with couples.*

1. Go back and review the stories of Immaculée Ilibagiza, Everett Worthington, and Marietta Jaeger. What was your initial reaction to their stories, and to the fact that they forgave the perpetrators? What do you find personally inspiring or challenging, and why?

2. Read and discuss the parable of the unforgiving servant in Matthew 18:21-35. Insert yourself imaginatively into the story: *you* are the debtor. Can you feel the impossible weight of your debt? The freedom that results from the king's mercy? What, by virtue of that mercy, has changed or should change about your attitude and behavior toward others?

3. Consider Chapman and Thomas' idea of the languages of apology: regret, responsibility, restitution, repentance, and

requesting. Does one resonate with you more than the others?

- If you're discussing this in a group, tell a story about how an apology that you made or that was made to you fell flat, and how things could have been done differently with a more fitting language of apology.

- If you're discussing this as couple, find a calm and undistracted time (most importantly, *not* when you're still stewing over something!) to tell similar stories and help each other understand the kind of apology that is most meaningful to you.

4. As Everett Worthington has said, forgiveness is "for giving, not for getting." Respond to that statement. Imagine moving from the state of not wanting to forgive at all, to forgiving in order to feel better, to forgiving as a gift to the offender—and possibly even beginning to wish him or her well (again, cf. Matthew 5:43-48). With which of these three states do you most identify? Which would you like to be true of you, and why? And what would it take (or, possibly, "what has it taken") for you to get there?

5. Talk about the nine-step process described at the end of the chapter. For convenience, here are the steps again, in brief:

   - Accept the fact that we live in a sin-ridden world.
   - Accept the fact that there is sin and brokenness in your own marriage.
   - With compassion for yourself, recognize the ways in which you bring your own vulnerability and brokenness to the marriage.
   - Meditate on the gift of grace you have already received from God, and the grace you still need each day.

- Consider carefully what your identity as a Christian demands in this situation.
- Ask yourself whether you really desire God's peace.
- Make a decision as to what path you will pursue.
- Have compassion for your spouse.
- Give your spouse the gift of mercy.

Which of the steps seems easiest? Hardest? Most confusing? As a group, discuss each step; try to come to a shared consensus of what each one means and why it would be personally important. Then consider together what the group might be able to do to support and encourage one another in the pursuit of peace through apology and forgiveness.

9

EPILOGUE: WALKING TOGETHER

The previous chapter provided the final practical link in a chain of kingdom-oriented virtues. Peacemakers live in hope toward a glorious future promised by a gracious God, even as they hunger to see justice done in the present. In humility, they grieve the effects of sin and brokenness in all its forms, and seek to put what power they have in the service of making peace. And they strive to be consistent in compassion, whether through everyday empathy, repentant apology, or merciful forgiveness. But as I said at the end of chapter 3, we were not meant to be peacemakers by ourselves. We need people who will walk alongside us, encourage and strengthen us, and help us get back on our feet when we stumble. We need, in other words, congregations—not just individuals—committed to peace.

ꟸ

It may seem strange to end a Christian book about peacemaking and marriage with a story about the Dalai Lama, but bear with me.

Douglas Preston writes of a time when the Buddhist leader toured the United States. The year was 1991. The Dalai Lama had received the Nobel Peace Prize two years before, but had not yet achieved the rockstar status that would come later. At the time, Preston was a magazine writer earning a meager living, and was tapped by the event organizer to volunteer as press secretary.

While visiting a community of Tibetan refugees in New Mexico, the Dalai Lama made an unanticipated request: he wanted to be taken up into the mountains, because he had never seen people ski. He marveled at the spectacle, even laughing with delight when a group of startled teens accidentally barreled into his party, sending him and his monks sprawling into the snow.

Later, as the group relaxed at the ski lodge, a waitress stopped to listen in on their conversation. Tentatively, she ventured a question, indeed, *the* Question: "What is the meaning of life?" In his entire week with their distinguished visitor, Preston writes, no one had dared ask *that.* But the Dalai Lama didn't hesitate:

> "The meaning of life is *happiness.*" He raised his finger, leaning forward, focusing on her as if she were the only person in the world. "Hard question is not, 'What is meaning of life?' That is easy… No, hard question is what *make* happiness. Money? Big house? Accomplishment? Friends? Or…" He paused. "Compassion and good heart? This is question all human beings must try to answer: *What make true happiness*?" He gave this last question a peculiar emphasis and then fell silent, gazing at her with a smile.[1]

"What is the meaning of life?" In my imagination, I envision the waitress hovering on the edge of the conversational field, a sense of curiosity and spiritual longing awakened by Dalai Lama's presence. Until that moment, she may not even have realized the question buried inside her.

I can't help but wonder: what would happen if she brought that same yearning to a local gathering of those who claim to follow Jesus? How would the members of that congregation explain the meaning of life, or the nature of "true happiness"? And most importantly, would the truth of what they said be evidenced in the life of the community itself?

Given a choice, many of us might say we'd like to have a happier life in general, or a happier marriage in particular. There's nothing wrong with that. But as I've suggested throughout these pages, our true happiness—our blessedness—comes from the daily pursuit of the kingdom that Jesus inaugurated, taught, and lived. We seek to embody kingdom-oriented virtues, but not as a self-help strategy for cooling off marital conflict. Rather, we begin to reimagine ourselves as peacemakers, as those called to live out the story the Bible tells, a story of new life, of wholeness emerging from brokenness.

What kind of peace do we want in our homes? Is it just that we want to stop arguing with and nitpicking at each other? Certainly that's a move in the right direction. But God's peace is so much more. Being a peacemaker involves not just a change in behavior but a change of heart, of desire, of vision. Virtue isn't just good behavior done for its own sake; it springs from a spiritual longing that has been captivated by a vision of the good. James Smith has said it well:

> Our ultimate love is oriented by and to a picture of what we think it looks like to live well, and that picture then governs, shapes, and motivates our decisions and actions. ...Thus we become certain kinds of people; we begin to emulate, mimic, and mirror the particular vision that we desire. ...[T]o be human is to desire "the kingdom," some version of the kingdom, which is the aim of our quest.[2]

But is that quest for the kingdom—for peace—a solitary one? We sometimes think of the Christian life primarily in terms of our one-on-one relationship with God, and read the Bible as if it were meant solely for private study and reflection. Even in so-called "corporate" gatherings, we are typically left to our own individual thoughts and experiences. We may be sitting together, but functionally speaking, without a place for conversation and mutual encouragement, we might as well all be watching the same religious program from the comfort of our living rooms.

An exaggeration? Perhaps. And I'm not suggesting that worship services should include small group discussion (though that might shake things up a bit). But the very vitality of the virtues—hope and hunger, humility and compassion—depends on whether we can consistently understand ourselves as living inside God's story of redemption and peace. Amidst the ups and downs of life and marriage, that kind of imagination is difficult to sustain on our own. And we shouldn't have to, for the chapter of the story that we are in right now is not meant to be about heroic individuals, but God's new creation of a *people* of peace, a people who tell and retell the story to each other, who encourage one another to hold onto the vision of God's shalom. As Tod Bolsinger has written:

> A people of the story must know, know deeply, and know by heart the story. ...Think about how much more deeply our lives would be changed if families and friends together were sharing, talking about, and encouraging one another to live out the same texts.[3]

What does it mean to be a "people of the story"? N. T. Wright suggests the following parable. Imagine that someone discovers an unfinished play by Shakespeare. The first four acts are undoubtedly the master's work, and are so compelling that they demand to be performed. But the fifth act is incomplete. What to do? Contract a playwright to finish the fifth act? Probably not.

The better solution, Wright suggests, is to recruit a troupe of dedicated actors who know the corpus of Shakespeare's work inside and out, and who can therefore fully inhabit the first four acts in a way that enables them to work out a satisfying and appropriate fifth act together.

The first four acts of the biblical drama, Wright suggests, could be entitled Creation, Fall, Israel, and Jesus. And we have tantalizing glimpses of how the story will end—resurrection, glory, a new heaven and a new earth. But in the meantime, the church has its creative commission: "We are looking... for and at a vocation to be the people of God in the fifth act of the drama of creation."[4]

What would happen if we understood our calling as the people of God in this way? What would change about the way we understand the Christian life, and what it means to be a church?

We need each other. Think back to the story of Kitty Genovese from the beginning of chapter 7, and the notion of the so-called "bystander effect." Why do people seem to act so callously? How can they ignore such obvious suffering? It's not that people don't notice, nor is it necessarily that they don't care. But our compassion is mixed with self-protection; we're quite capable of saying to ourselves both "Do something!" and "Don't get involved!" at the same time. And even more poignantly, if we look around and see that no one else is doing anything, the self-protective voice wins, and we go on our way.

But if just one other person around us steps up to help, it can change everything. Suddenly we find the courage to do what we should have done in the first place.

We don't need people to side with our cynicism about marriage. We don't need places where we can do nothing more than complain and commiserate. Instead, we need to be surrounded by people who can envision the home as an arena for God's work of peace, who can encourage us to put our hope in God's faithfulness, to hunger for relational justice, to be living, breathing embodiments of divine humility and compassion. And we need to be those people ourselves, for the sake of others. That is the vocation of peacemakers and the calling of God's people *as* a people.

How we relate to each other matters, and matters deeply. I'm reminded of one my favorite quotes from C. S. Lewis, who in his characteristically insightful way helps us realize what it really means to live side by side with those created in God's image and possessing an eternal destiny:

> It is a serious thing to live in a society of possible gods and goddesses, to remember that the dullest and most uninteresting person you can talk to may one day be a creature which, if you saw it now, you would be strongly tempted to worship, or else a horror and a corruption such as you now meet, if at all, only in a nightmare. All day long we

> are, in some degree, helping each other to one or other of these destinations. It is in the light of these overwhelming possibilities, it is with the awe and the circumspection proper to them, that we should conduct all our dealings with one another, all friendships, all loves, all play, all politics. There are no ordinary people. You have never talked to a mere mortal. Nations, cultures, arts, civilisations—these are mortal, and their life is to ours as the life of a gnat. But it is immortals whom we joke with, work with, marry, snub, and exploit—immortal horrors or everlasting splendors.[5]

Is that how we see each other in our marriages, in our churches? Lewis wants us to understand that whether we recognize it or not, we are constantly shaping one another through our relationships, as we all make our way toward our final destination. The choices we make have consequences.

Let us therefore choose to walk the path of peace, together.

℘଼

Questions for discussion and reflection:

1. What kind of conversations about marriage are you used to having at church? I don't mean listening to a sermon about marriage, but how you and other members of the congregation actually talk about life at home. In what ways, if at all, do these conversations encourage or discourage hope, hunger, humility, and compassion? What would you change, and how?

2. Reread and respond to the quote from C. S. Lewis. Can you imagine your spouse as someone created in the image of God, someone with an eternal destiny? What might it mean to envision him or her as an "immortal horror" or an "everlasting splendor"—and to know that you have a role in shaping that destiny?

3. Peacemaking is not merely an individual pursuit. We need the support and encouragement of a community that purposes to live God's story together. Imagine together what that might look like in your church. Toward that end, what one or two things might you do differently together as a body?

NOTES

Introduction

1 See, e.g., John M. Gottman, *The Marriage Clinic: A Scientifically-Based Marital Therapy* (New York, NY: W. W. Norton, 1999), and more recently, John M. Gottman, *The Science of Trust: Emotional Attunement for Couples* (New York, NY: W. W. Norton, 2011).

Chapter 1: The Pursuit of Happiness

1 As with other couples mentioned in the book, Danny and Celia are a fictional composite of couples I have known or worked with.

2 Daniel Gilbert, *Stumbling on Happiness* (New York, NY: Vintage Books, 2007), chapter 4.

3 The term "hedonic treadmill" originated with P. Brickman and D. T. Campbell, "Hedonic Relativism and Planning the Good Society," in *Adaptation Level Theory: A Symposium*, ed. Mortimer H. Appley (New York, NY: Academic Press, 1971): 287-302.

4 See, e.g., Roy F. Baumeister, Ellen Bratslavsky, Catrin Finkenauer, and Kathleen D. Vohs, "Bad is Stronger than Good," *Review of General Psychology* 5 (2001): 323-370; Seligman, *Authentic Happiness*, p. 49.

5 E.g., "The Tragic Stories of the Lottery's Unluckiest Winners," including Billie Bob Harrell, Jr., who committed suicide in 1999, not long after winning a $31 million Lotto jackpot. Harrell was quoted as saying, "Winning the lottery is the worst thing that ever happened to me." See http://newsfeed.time.com/2012/11/28/500-million-powerball-jackpot-the-tragic-stories-of-the-lotterys-unluckiest-winners/.

6 Daniel Kahneman and Angus Deaton, "High Income Improves Evaluation of Life But Not Emotional Well-Being," *Proceedings of*

the National Academy of Sciences 107 (2010): 16489-16493.

7 Sonja Lyubomirsky, *The How of Happiness: A New Approach to Getting the Life you Want* (New York, NY: Penguin, 2007), p. 41.

8 Lyubomirsky, *How of Happiness*, pp. 52-62; Martin E. P. Seligman, *Authentic Happiness: Using the New Positive Psychology to Realize Your Potential for Lasting Fulfillment* (New York, NY: The Free Press, 2002), pp. 47-48.

9 Lyubomirsky, *How of Happiness*, p. 53.

10 For example, Ed Diener, perhaps the best known researcher of happiness and subjective well-being, has suggested that if people do have set points, they may change over time, and the same person may have one set point for positive emotion, and another for negative emotion. See Ed Diener, Richard E. Lucas, and Christie Napa Scollon, "Beyond the Hedonic Treadmill: Revising the Adaptation Theory of Well-Being," *American Psychologist* 61 (2006): 305-314.

11 These are among the twelve practical "happiness activities" suggested by Lyubomirsky, *How of Happiness,* chapters 4 through 9.

12 Martin E. P. Seligman, *Flourish: A Visionary New Understanding of Happiness and Well-Being* (New York, NY: The Free Press, 2011), pp. 9-10. Positive psychology is a relatively recent approach to research, theory, and treatment that focuses more on health than pathology, and is committed to understanding and increasing well-being instead of merely reducing symptoms. The title Seligman wanted for his 2002 book, *Authentic Happiness*, was *Positive Psychology*; the publisher insisted that the word "happiness" would be more marketable. (They were probably right.)

13 Seligman, *Flourish*, pp. 16-26.

14 Mihaly Csikszentmihalyi, *Flow: The Psychology of Optimal Experience* (New York, NY: Harper Perennial, 1990).

15 Seligman, *Authentic Happiness*, chapter 9.

16 Seligman, *Authentic Happiness,* p. 130.

17 Seligman, *Flourish*, p. 264-265. Short, self-scoring versions of the *Signature Strengths Test* can be found in both *Authentic Happiness* and *Flourish*; adult and child versions of Seligman's *VIA Strengths Survey* (and other measures) can be accessed online at http://www.authentichappiness.com.

18 E.g., Linda Waite and Maggie Gallagher, *The Case for Marriage* (New York, NY: Broadway Books, 2001).

19 Lyubomirsky, *How of Happiness*, p. 49. The study of 1,761 people was conducted in Germany. A recent study of British households adds that marriage may help protect a person from a long-term decline in life satisfaction. But even if life satisfaction goes up after the wedding, it returns to its premarital level soon after the first year. See Stevie C. Y. Yap, Ivana Anusic, and Richard E. Lucas, "Does Personality Moderate Reaction and Adaptation to Major Life Events? Evidence from the British Household Panel Survey," *Journal of Research in Personality* 46 (2012): 477-488.

20 Blaine Fowers, *Beyond the Myth of Marital Happiness: How Embracing the Virtues of Loyalty, Generosity, Justice, and Courage Can Strengthen Your Relationship* (San Francisco, CA: Jossey-Bass, 2000), p. 10.

21 Fowers, *Beyond the Myth of Marital Happiness*, pp. 10, 23.

22 Noah Webster, *An American Dictionary of the English Language* (New York, NY: S. Converse, 1828).

23 Philip Yancey, *The Bible Jesus Read* (Grand Rapids, MI: Zondervan, 1999).

24 Not "Herod the Great" of the Christmas story in Matthew 2, but his son by his fourth wife, Malthace. The half-brother in question was Herod Philip, son of his third wife, Mariamne. His second wife was also named Mariamne. And you thought *you* had a complicated family.

25 Blaine Fowers, *Virtue and Psychology: Pursuing Excellence in Ordinary Practices* (Washington, DC: American Psychological Association, 2005), p. 29.

26 Jonathan Haidt, *The Happiness Hypothesis: Finding Modern Truth in Ancient Wisdom* (New York, NY: Basic Books, 2006), p. 238.

27 Glen H. Stassen and David P. Gushee, *Kingdom Ethics: Following Jesus in Contemporary Context* (Downers Grove, IL: InterVarsity Press, 2003), p. 51.

Chapter 2: Making Peace

1 "Say what you want, not what you don't want" is a key principle taught in the well-known Family Wellness curriculum *Survival Skills*

for Healthy Families. See Flo Creighton and George Doub, *Family Wellness Instructor Manual* (Scotts Valley, CA: Family Wellness Associates, 1999), session 3. See also Virginia Scott, George Doub, and Peggy Runnels, *Raising a Loving Family* (Holbrook, MA: Adams Media, 1999), p. 6.

2 Ken Sande and Tom Raabe, *Peacemaking for Families: A Biblical Guide to Managing Conflict in Your Home* (Carol Stream, IL: Tyndale, 2002), pp. ix, 10. Sande's work focuses much more on specific strategies for biblically-based conflict resolution.

3 Andy Crouch, *Playing God: Redeeming the Gift of Power* (Downers Grove, IL: InterVarsity, 2013), p. 29.

4 Cornelius Plantinga, *Not the Way It's Supposed to Be: A Breviary of Sin* (Grand Rapids, MI: Eerdmans, 1995), p. 10.

5 David Gushee, *Getting Marriage Right: Realistic Counsel for Saving and Strengthening Relationships* (Grand Rapid, MI: Baker Books, 2004), p. 94. "Marriage," writes Gushee, "is for companionship" in work, daily living, and love (pp. 94-95).

6 Gwyneth Paltrow, "Conscious Uncoupling," posted March 25, 2014, at http://goop.com/journal/ be/conscious-uncoupling.

7 See "Dr. Habib Sadeghi & Dr. Sherry Sami on Conscious Uncoupling," at URL in note above.

8 Glen Stassen, *Living the Sermon on the Mount* (San Francisco, CA: Jossey-Bass, 2006), p. 65.

9 Stassen, *Sermon on the Mount*, p. 65.

10 Cameron Lee, *Unexpected Blessing: Living the Countercultural Reality of the Beatitudes* (Downers Grove, IL: InterVarsity, 2004), chapter 8.

11 John Paul Lederach, *The Moral Imagination: The Art and Soul of Building Peace* (New York, NY: Oxford, 2005), especially chapter 4. The four characteristics are paraphrased.

12 E.g. Sande and Raabe, *Peacemaking for Families*, cited earlier.

13 This is known in Roman Catholic canon law as the "Pauline Privilege," by which a marriage can legitimately be dissolved if (1) both partners were unbaptized when they married, (2) one later becomes baptized, and (3) the other neither wishes to be baptized nor to remain in the marriage.

14 As told in Lee Strobel and Leslie Strobel, *Surviving a Spiritual Mismatch in Marriage* (Grand Rapids, MI: Zondervan, 2002). The story, as many Christian readers know, has a happy ending: Lee

eventually became a Christian.

15 Stassen, *Sermon on the Mount,* pp. 75-78. He notes that Jesus' teaching regarding divorce in Matthew 5:31-32 is unaccompanied by a transforming initiative, unlike the teachings regarding murder/anger and adultery/lust. He regards Paul's command to be reconciled in 1 Corinthians 7:10-11 as providing the missing piece, under the authority of Jesus.

16 Ron Martoia, *The Bible as Improv* (Grand Rapids, MI: Zondervan, 2010), p. 174.

17 Martoia, *Bible as Improv,* p. 198.

Chapter 3: Every Marriage Needs Hope

1 J. R. R. Tolkien, *The Two Towers* (New York, NY: Ballantine, 1965), p. 407.

2 J. R. R. Tolkien, *The Return of the King* (New York, NY: Ballantine, 1965), p. 281.

3 Howard J. Markman, Scott M. Stanley, and Susan L. Blumberg, *Fighting for Your Marriage: Positive Steps for Preventing Divorce and Preserving a Lasting Love,* rev. ed. (San Francisco, CA: Jossey-Bass, 2001), p. 191.

4 See "Love in the Movies," a special featurette included with the film's 10th anniversary DVD release.

5 Thomas Moore, *Soul Mates: Honoring the Mysteries of Love and Relationship* (New York, NY: HarperPerennial, 1994), p. xvii.

6 Barbara D. Whitehead and David Popenoe, "Who Wants to Marry a Soul Mate?", pp. 6, 8. See the Project's 2001 report, *The State of Our Unions 2001: The Social Health of Marriage in America*, available online at http://www.stateofourunions.org/pdfs/SOOU2001.pdf.

7 Mali Apple and Joe Dunn, *The Soulmate Experience: A Practical Guide to Creating Extraordinary Relationships* (San Rafael, CA: A Higher Possibility, 2011), p. 69. "Soulmates" (as a single word) is the authors' spelling.

8 David E. Garland and Diana R. Garland, *Flawed Families of the Bible: How God's Grace Works through Imperfect Relationships* (Grand Rapids, MI: Brazos Press, 2007), p. 50.

9 Walter Brueggemann, *Biblical Perspectives on Evangelism: Living in a*

Three-Storied Universe (Nashville, TN: Abingdon Press, 1993), pp. 108-109.

10 Eric and Leslie Ludy, *When God Writes Your Love Story: The Ultimate Approach to Guy/Girl Relationships* (Sisters, OR: Loyal Publishing, 1999), pp. 57-58.

11 Ludy and Ludy, *When God Writes Your Love Story*, p. 62. Despite this emphasis, remnants of the romantic ideal still seem to remain in the book.

12 Hannah Wegmann, "My Husband is Not My Soul Mate," at http://theartinlife.wordpress.com/2013/07/22/my-husband-is-not-my-soul-mate/; emphasis in original. A few months later, Seth Adam Smith's blog post "Marriage Isn't For You" (see http://sethadamsmith.com/2013/11/02/marriage-isnt-for-you/), which included advice from *his* father, also went viral. For my response to Smith, see http://the-fog-blog.com/2014/02/14/happy-valentines-day/.

13 Cameron Lee, *Beyond Family Values: A Call to Christian Virtue* (Downers Grove, IL: InterVarsity, 1998), chapters 7 and 8.

14 N. T. Wright, *Surprised by Hope: Rethinking Heaven, the Resurrection, and the Mission of the Church* (New York, NY: HarperOne, 2008), pp. 208-209.

15 Shane Lopez, *Making Hope Happen* (New York, NY: Atria Books, 2013), p. 129. Elsewhere in the book, however, Lopez does recognize the power of relationships to either encourage or discourage hope.

16 Nicholas A. Christakis and James H. Fowler, *Connected: The Surprising Power of Our Social Networks and How They Shape Our Lives* (New York, NY: Little, Brown, 2009), pp. 27-28.

Chapter 4: Hungering for the Right Things

1 E.g. Paco Underhill, *Why We Buy: The Science of Shopping* (New York, NY: Simon and Schuster, 2000).

2 Eric Schlosser, *Fast Food Nation: The Dark Side of the All-American Meal* (New York, NY: Houghton Mifflin, 2001), p. 43.

3 The research was done at Cornell University; see Aviva Musicus, Aner Tal, and Brian Wansink, "Eyes in the Aisles: Why is Cap'n

Crunch Looking Down at My Child?" A summary by Katherine Baildon is available online at http://foodpsychology.cornell.edu/op/cerealeyes.

4 James B. Adamson, for example, notes that the Greek words for "envy" and "kill/murder" are quite similar, and suggests that "envy" might have been the original reading. See his commentary, *The Epistle of James* (Grand Rapids, MI: Eerdmans, 1976), p. 168.

5 See, e.g., Scott M. Stanley, Howard J. Markman, and Sarah W. Whitton, "Communication, Conflict, and Commitment: Insights on the Foundations of Relationship Success from a National Survey," *Family Process* 41 (2002): 659-675.

6 Cameron Lee and James L. Furrow, *Preparing Couples for Love and Marriage: A Pastor's Resource* (Nashville, TN: Abingdon, 2013).

7 Robert Sternberg, *Love is a Story* (New York, NY: Oxford, 1998), p. 7.

8 FAO, IFAD, and WFP, *The State of Food Insecurity in the World 2013: The Multiple Dimensions of Food Security* (Rome: FAO, 2013), p. 2. Report available online at http://wfpusa.org/sites/default/files/resources/fao_insecurity_report_2013_text.pdf.

9 See the website of Lifewater International: http://lifewater.org/crisis/.

10 The various versions of the feeding of the 5,000 are found in Matthew 14:13-21, Mark 6:32-44, Luke 9:10-17, and John 6:1-13. The description here combines elements of different accounts.

11 Søren Kierkegaard, *Purity of Heart is to Will One Thing,* trans. Douglas V. Steere (New York, NY: Harper Torchbooks, 1956).

12 Eugene Peterson, *A Long Obedience in the Same Direction: Discipleship in an Instant Society,* 2nd ed. (Downers Grove, IL: InterVarsity Press, 2000). The phrase is borrowed from Friedrich Nietzsche's *Beyond Good and Evil,* which Peterson quotes on p. 13.

13 *The Book of Common Prayer and Administration of the Sacraments and Other Rites and Ceremonies of the Church* (New York, NY: Oxford University Press, 1928), p. 301.

14 Scott Stanley, *The Heart of Commitment* (Nashville, TN: Thomas Nelson, 1998), chapter 1.

15 Stanley, *The Heart of Commitment,* p. 11.

16 See Stanley, et al., "Communication, Conflict, and Commitment," p. 660: "a clear and consistent commitment allows both partners to

feel secure and act in the relationship in ways that are only rational in the context of that security."

17 Compared to married people who have never divorced, individuals who have divorced and remarried are more likely to seek divorce when they encounter marital problems; see Sarah W. Whitton, Scott M. Stanley, Howard J. Markman, and Christine A. Johnson, "Attitudes Toward Divorce, Commitment, and Divorce Proneness in First Marriages and Remarriages," *Journal of Marriage and Family* 75 (2013): 276-287. Moreover, engaged women whose parents were divorced were less committed to and less confident in their current relationship; Sarah W. Whitton, Galena K. Rhoades, Scott M. Stanley, and Howard J. Markman, "Effects on Parental Divorce on Marital Commitment and Confidence," *Journal of Family Psychology* 22 (2008): 789-793.

Chapter 5: Grace to the Humble

1 Lederach, *The Moral Imagination,* p. 9.

2 Lederach, *The Moral Imagination*, p. 10.

3 Brett G. Scharffs, "Relational Humility," *Interdisciplinary Humanities* 30 (2013): 30.

4 Scharffs, "Relational Humility," p. 31. Indeed, Aristotle viewed pride as the "crown of the virtues." The word he uses can be translated "greatness of soul," the idea being that there are truly noble people who deserve honor and know it, without either over- or underestimating their worth (the latter being "undue humility"). See his *Nicomachean Ethics*, book IV, section 3. There is, it seems, only a short step from here to Nietzsche.

5 R. T. Kendall, *The Power of Humility* (Lake Mary, FL: Charisma House, 2011), Kindle edition, locations 156, 186. Emphasis added.

6 This is one of the central themes of Andy Crouch's meditation on power, *Playing God*, cited earlier.

7 Andrew Murray, *Humility*, Kindle edition, locations 76-77, 92-94. Originally published 1895.

8 E.g., John R. Means, Gregory L. Wilson, Cynthia Sturm, Joseph E. Bironi, and Paul J. Bach, "Humility as a Psycho-therapeutic Formulation," *Counseling Psychology Quarterly* 3 (1990): 211-215.

9 William C. Placher, *Narratives of a Vulnerable God: Christ, Theology, and Scripture* (Louisville, KY: Westminster John Knox, 1994), p. 58.

10 Robert C. Roberts, *Spiritual Emotions: A Psychology of Christian Virtues* (Grand Rapids, MI: Eerdmans, 2007), p. 83.

Chapter 6: At Home with Humility

1 Murray, *Humility*, Kindle location 78.

2 C. S. Lewis, *Mere Christianity* (New York, NY: HarperCollins, 2001), p. 129. Originally published 1952.

3 David G. Myers, "Humility: Theology Meets Psychology," *Reformed Review* 48 (1995): 195-206.

4 In the verses cited, the CEB translates various forms of the Greek verb *kauchaomai* (brag, boast, rejoice) as "proud."

5 C. S. Lewis, *The Screwtape Letters* (New York, NY: Touchstone, 1996), p. 59. Originally published 1942.

6 Cf., e.g., Terry D. Cooper, *Sin, Pride & Self-Acceptance: The Problem of Identity in Theology and Psychology* (Downers Grove, IL: InterVarsity Press, 2003).

7 Everett L. Worthington, Jr., *Humility: The Quiet Virtue* (Philadelphia, PA: Templeton Foundation Press, 2007), Kindle edition, location 62.

8 Terry D. Hargrave, *The Essential Humility of Marriage: Honoring the Third Identity in Couple Therapy* (Phoenix, AZ: Zeig, Tucker, & Theisen, 2000), p. x.

9 Hargrave, *The Essential Humility of Marriage*, pp. 6, 7, 9. The concept draws on the work of family therapist Carl Whitaker, and is similar to the concept of the "we" in romantic love as described by philosopher Robert Nozick, in "Love's Bond," in *The Examined Life: Philosophical Meditations* (New York, NY: Touchstone, 1989), pp. 68-86.

10 E.g., June Price Tangney, "Humility: Theoretical Perspectives, Empirical Findings and Directions for Future Research," *Journal of Social and Clinical Psychology* 19 (2000): 70-82.

11 Some studies, lacking a viable alternative, have actually done this. For example, study participants have been given the prompt, "I see myself as…" and then asked to rate themselves on a 7-point scale

with "arrogant" on end and "humble" on the other, raising the question of how a truly humble person should respond. See Annette Peters, Wade C. Rowatt, and Megan K. Johnson, "Associations between Dispositional Humility and Social Relationship Quality," *Psychology* 2 (2011): 156. It should also be noted, however, that most studies, including this one, attempt to account statistically for the influence of other personality traits and social desirability (the tendency of participants to give what they consider to be more socially valued responses) in their results.

12 Julie J. Exline and Peter C. Hill, "Humility: A Consistent and Robust Predictor of Generosity," *The Journal of Positive Psychology* 7 (2012): 208-218.

13 Jordan Paul LaBouff, Wade C. Rowatt, Megan K. Johnson, Jo-Ann Tsang, and Grace McCullough Willerton, "Humble Persons are More Helpful than Less Humble Persons: Evidence from Three Studies," *The Journal of Positive Psychology* 7 (2012): 16-29.

14 Julie J. Exline, "Humility and the Ability to Receive from Others," *Journal of Psychology and Christianity* 31 (2012): 40-50.

15 Peters, Rowatt, and Johnson, "Associations between Dispositional Humility and Social Relationship Quality."

16 June Price Tangney, "Humility," in *Oxford Handbook of Positive Psychology,* ed. Shane J. Lopez and C. R. Snyder, 483-490 (New York, NY: Oxford University Press, 2009), p. 488.

17 Exline, "Humility and the Ability to Receive from Others," p. 41.

18 Tangney, "Humility," p. 485. I've paraphrased Tangney's wording, and reordered the points.

19 Here, I am leaving aside the matter of clinical depression, which introduces other elements.

20 See, e.g., Lee and Furrow, *Preparing Couples for Love and Marriage*, pp. 41-45.

21 Markman, et al., *Fighting for Your Marriage*, pp. 93-99. This is a paraphrase of the communication "filters" which they call *distractions*, *emotional states*, *beliefs and expectations*, and *differences in style*.

22 This is the skill known as "Power Listening Lite" in the marriage curriculum known as World Class Marriage. See Patty Howell and Ralph Jones, *World Class Marriage: How to Create the Relationship You Always Wanted with the Partner You Already Have* (Lanham, MD:

Rowman & Littlefield, 2010), pp. 33-42.

23 Andrew Butcher, "In My Humble Opinion," *Stimulus: The New Zealand Journal of Christian Thought and Practice* 19, no. 3 (2012): 42.

24 John Gottman and Nan Silver, *The Seven Principles for Making Marriage Work* (New York, NY: Three Rivers Press, 1999), pp. 99-128.

25 Caroline J. Simon, *The Disciplined Heart: Love, Destiny, and Imagination* (Grand Rapids, MI: Eerdmans, 1997), p. 65.

26 Many marriage curricula teach communication and listening skills. If there are no classes or workshops in your area, here are some resources with which to begin: Markman, et al., *Fighting for Your Marriage*, cited earlier; Michael P. Nichols, *The Lost Art of Listening* (New York, NY: Guilford, 2009); Douglas Stone, Bruce Patton, and Sheila Heen, *Difficult Conversations: How to Discuss What Matters Most,* updated ed. (New York, NY: Penguin, 2010).

Chapter 7: The Compassion Connection

1 The details of the case are drawn from a *New Yorker* book review by Nicholas Lemann, entitled "A Call for Help: What the Kitty Genovese Story Really Means." Posted online March 10, 2014, at http://www.newyorker.com/arts/critics/books/2014/03/10/140310crbo_books_lemann?currentPage=all. Lemann is reviewing two recent books: Kevin Cook, *Kitty Genovese: The Murder, the Bystanders, and the Crime that Changed America* (New York, NY: W. W. Norton, 2014), and Catherine Pelonero, *Kitty Genovese: A True Account of a Public Murder and its Private Consequences* (New York, NY : Skyhorse Publishing, 2014).

2 There are many compelling videos of the bystander effect on YouTube, e.g., https://www.youtube.com/watch?v=OSsPfbup0ac.

3 It is possible to construe certain biblical passages this way. In context, however, the concern usually seems to be with the purity, holiness, and obedience of God's people, not with social or ethnic distinctions.

4 The verb in the Greek is *splanchnizomai*, from the noun *splanchna*, which means "entrails," or in colloquial English, "guts."

5 The point is made by Joel Green, *The Gospel of Luke* (Grand Rapids,

MI: Eerdmans, 1997), p. 432. The Samaritan would likely be cheated.

6 Henri Nouwen, Donald P. McNeill, and Douglas A. Morrison, *Compassion: A Reflection on the Christian Life* (New York, NY: Image, 1982), p. 14.

7 See also 2 Chronicles 30:9 and Nehemiah 9:31.

8 Sonja Lyubomirsky, "Happiness for a Lifetime," posted July 15, 2010, at http://greatergood.berkeley.edu/article/item/happiness_for_a_lifetime/.

9 Lori Gordon and Jon Frandsen, *Passage to Intimacy,* rev. ed. (no publisher: 2000), pp. 238-239.

10 The literature on the subject is voluminous. A good starting point is the work of Daniel J. Siegel, who has written for both professional and general audiences. Two examples of the former are *The Developing Mind* (New York, NY: Guilford, 1999) and *Pocket Guide to Interpersonal Neurobiology: An Integrative Handbook of the Mind* (New York, NY: W. W. Norton, 2012). Examples of the latter are *Mindsight: The New Science of Personal Transformation* (New York, NY: Bantam, 2011) and *Brainstorm: The Power and Purpose of the Teenage Brain* (New York, NY: Penguin, 2013). Because much of what is now known about the neurobiology of the brain is common knowledge across the literature, I will only cite specific sources when quoting or referencing particular works.

11 Bonnie Badenoch, *Being a Brain-Wise Therapist: A Practical Guide to Interpersonal Neurobiology* (New York, NY: W. W. Norton, 2008), p. 25.

12 Gordon and Frandsen, *Passage to Intimacy,* pp. 35-36.

13 This describes what Lori Gordon calls this the "emotional allergy infinity loop"; see Gordon and Frandsen, *Passage to Intimacy,* chapter 18. Mona DeKoven Fishbane calls it the "vulnerability cycle"; see Fishbane, *Loving with the Brain in Mind: Neurobiology and Couple Therapy* (New York, NY: W. W. Norton, 2013), chapter 7.

14 Eric J. Cassell, "Compassion," in *Oxford Handbook of Positive Psychology,* ed. Lopez and Snyder, p. 395.

15 Gottman, *The Science of Trust,* pp. 195-196.

16 Andrew Christensen and Neil S. Jacobson, *Reconcilable Differences* (New York, NY: Guilford, 2000), chapter 6. Each need and personal statement that follows the bullet is quoted directly from

Christensen and Jacobson; the descriptions of each are in my words.

17 Fishbane, *Loving with the Brain in Mind,* Kindle edition, location 2462.

Chapter 8: Mercy is For Giving

1 Immaculée Ilibagiza (with Steve Erwin), *Left to Tell: Discovering God Amidst the Rwandan Holocaust* (Carlsbad, CA: Hay House, 2006), p. 204.

2 Ilibagiza, *Left to Tell,* p. 204.

3 Ilibagiza, *Left to Tell,* p. 94.

4 The observation is made in several commentaries, e.g., Donald A. Hagner, *Matthew 14-28* (Nashville, TN: Thomas Nelson, 1995), p. 537.

5 The Greek word is *homologeo*, which literally means to "say the same thing"—in this context, it suggests an outward agreement with the inner conviction of the Holy Spirit.

6 In James, the verb is *exomologeo*, an intensified form of *homologeo* that suggests an outward, public confession.

7 Gary Chapman and Jennifer Thomas, *When Sorry Isn't Enough: Making Things Right with Those You Love* (Chicago, IL: Northfield Publishing, 2013). This is an updated version of an earlier work, Chapman and Thomas, *The Five Languages of Apology* (Chicago, IL: Northfield Publishing, 2006).

8 According to their own informal research, 75% of couples differ on their preferred language of apology. Chapman and Thomas, *When Sorry Isn't Enough*, p. 84.

9 The questions are adapted from Chapman and Thomas, *When Sorry Isn't Enough*, pp. 84-87. The book also contains an "apology language profile" for self-test purposes.

10 Gary Chapman, *The Five Love Languages: The Secret to Love that Lasts* (Chicago, IL: Northfield Publishing, 2010).

11 Chapman and Thomas, *When Sorry Isn't Enough*, p. 59.

12 Adapted from Chapman and Thomas, *When Sorry Isn't Enough*, pp. 61-69.

13 Everett Worthington, *Forgiving and Reconciling: Bridges to Wholeness*

and Hope (Downers Grove, IL: InterVarsity Press, 2003), p. 19.

14 See, for example, Kathryn Belicki, Nancy DeCourville, Kerri Michalica, and Tammy Stewart, "Differences in Why People Forgive, and Why It Matters," *Family and Community Ministries* 26 (2013): 26-48, in which the researchers suggest on empirical grounds that forgiveness based on mere religious obligation is often ineffective.

15 Anne Lamott, *Traveling Mercies: Some Thoughts on Faith* (New York, NY: Anchor, 1999), p. 134.

16 See, for example, Edward M. Hallowell, *Dare to Forgive* (Deerfield Beach, FL: Health Communications, 2004), which includes chapters entitled, "Forgiveness is a Gift You Give to Yourself," and "Forgiveness Sets You Free." To be fair, we should note that Hallowell is aware of both sides of the forgiveness equation: "Forgiveness is a gift you give to others, but it is also a gift you give to *yourself*" (p. 12, emphasis in original).

17 On rumination, see Barbara L. Fredrickson, *Positivity* (New York, NY: Three Rivers Press, 2009), pp. 163-166.

18 Hallowell, *Dare to Forgive,* p. 7. Psychologist Robert D. Enright has also conducted numerous studies on the personal benefits of forgiveness training. For a summary of his empirical results, see Enright, *The Forgiving Life: A Pathway to Overcoming Resentment and Creating a Legacy of Love* (Washington, DC: American Psychological Association, 2012), table 2.1, Kindle location 453-457.

19 Quoted in Hallowell, *Dare to Forgive,* p. 234.

20 Quoted in Hallowell, *Dare to Forgive,* pp. 238-239.

21 Worthington, *Forgiving and Reconciling*, p. 26.

22 Worthington, *Forgiving and Reconciling*, p. 26.

23 Martin Luther King, *Stride Toward Freedom: The Montgomery Story* (Bostson, MA: Beacon Press, 2010), p. 208. A slightly different version of the saying is commonly attributed to Mahatma Gandhi.

24 Miroslav Volf, *Free of Charge: Giving and Forgiving in a Culture Stripped of Grace* (Grand Rapids, MI: Zondervan, 2005), p. 140.

25 Lynn Darling, "For Better and Worse," in *Here Lies My Heart,* eds. Deborah Chasman and Catherine Jhee, 178-202 (Boston, MA: Beacon Press, 1999), p. 189.

26 This is a variation on what is known as "the miracle question" in solution-focused therapy. See, e.g., Steve de Shazer and Yvonne

Dolan, *More than Miracles: The State of the Art of Solution-Focused Brief Therapy* (New York, NY: Haworth Press, 2007), chapter 3.

27 Eugene Peterson, *A Long Obedience in the Same Direction: Discipleship in an Instant Society,* 20th anniversary ed. (Downers Grove, IL: InterVarsity Press, 2000). The phrase is actually borrowed from Friedrich Nietzsche's *Beyond Good and Evil.*

28 Hallowell, *Dare to Forgive,* p. 87.

29 Robert D. Enright, *Forgiveness is a Choice: A Step-By-Step Process for Resolving Anger and Restoring Hope* (Washington, DC: American Psychological Association, 2008), p. 25.

30 Enright, *Forgiveness is a Choice*, p. 39.

Epilogue: Walking Together

1 Douglas Preston, "The Dalai Lama's Ski Trip," published February 26, 2014 on Slate.com: http://www.slate.com/articles/life/culturebox/2014/02/dalai_lama_at_a_santa_fe_ski_resort_tells_waitress_the_meaning_of_life.html.

2 James K. A. Smith, *Desiring the Kingdom: Worship, Worldview, and Cultural Formation* (Grand Rapids, MI: Baker Books, 2009), pp. 53-54.

3 Tod E. Bolsinger, *It Takes a Church to Raise a Christian: How the Community of God Transforms Lives* (Grand Rapids, MI: Brazos Press, 2004), pp. 131-133.

4 N. T. Wright, *The New Testament and the People of God* (Minneapolis, MN: Fortress Press, 1992), p. 142. His use of the Shakespearean drama metaphor begins on p. 140; his outline of the first four acts of the biblical drama appears on p. 141. It should be noted that others have proposed similar dramatic schemes; for a general reading audience, I would recommend beginning with John Eldredge, *Epic: The Story God is Telling* (Nashville, TN: Thomas Nelson, 2004).

5 C. S. Lewis, *The Weight of Glory* (New York, NY: HarperCollins, 2001), pp. 45-46, emphasis added.

ABOUT THE AUTHOR

Cameron Lee, PhD, CFLE, is Professor of Family Studies and the founder of the Fuller Institute for Relationship Education (FIRE) at Fuller Theological Seminary in Pasadena, California, where he has taught since 1986. As a licensed minister, Certified Family Life Educator, and trainer for Family Wellness, he regularly conducts workshops on marriage and family life, primarily in church-related settings. He is the senior or sole author of six previous books, most recently *That Their Work Will Be a Joy: Understanding and Coping with the Challenges of Pastoral Ministry* (with Kurt Fredrickson, 2012), and *Preparing Couples for Love and Marriage: A Pastor's Resource* (with James L. Furrow, 2013). Cameron's blog on the Christian life, *Squinting through Fog*, can be found at http://the-fog-blog.com. He and his wife Suha have been married since 1978, and have two grown children. His diverse range of hobbies includes blogging, collecting Starbucks city mugs, digital photography, designing and decorating *pysanky* (Ukrainian Easter eggs), imitating Elvis, and fending off questions about his age.

Made in the USA
Charleston, SC
05 February 2015